THE HOLLYWOOD
PROFESSIONALS

Volume Three:

Howard Hawks
Frank Borzage
Edgar G. Ulmer

by
John Belton

This series spotlights the work of the many
professional directors at work in Hollywood during its heyday—talents who might otherwise be
ignored by film students and historians. John
Belton has contributed monographs and very
detailed filmographies of Howard Hawks, Frank
Borzage, and Edgar G. Ulmer, who between
them made scores of familiar movies with a competence and a gloss now rarely seen in the
cinema.

£1.25

In the same series,
produced by THE TANTIVY PRESS
and edited by Peter Cowie:

The Hollywood Professionals

HOWARD HAWKS
FRANK BORZAGE
EDGAR G. ULMER

by

John Belton

THE TANTIVY PRESS, LONDON
A. S. BARNES & CO., NEW YORK

Acknowledgements

I would like to acknowledge my indebtedness to the writings of Fred Camper on Howard Hawks and Frank Borzage and those of Mike Prokosch on Edgar G. Ulmer. My wife, Ellen, and my friend, Marty Lubin, were extremely helpful in editing and revising each of the three essays. I would like to thank Tim Hunter, Mike Prokosch and Geoff Modest of Harvard Film Studies for providing me, over the years, with great American films to see, including many directed by Hawks, Borzage and Ulmer. I would also like to thank Robert Smith and Jeffrey L. Wise of the University of Connecticut at Storrs, Conn., for their Borzage retrospective and Ron Collier of Bennett College, Milbrook, N.Y., for his help in screening Ulmer films. Tony Slide of the American Film Institute was of great assistance in locating stills and in compiling the Borzage filmography. The Wisconsin Center for Theater Research aided me in seeing a number of films. My thanks to "Monogram" and "The Velvet Light Trap" for permission to reprint expanded and revised versions of my articles on Borzage and Ulmer. One of my students, John Williams, influenced my ideas on *The Big Sleep.* My final thanks to Shirley Ulmer who supplied me many stills and much information about her husband, Edgar. Other illustrations courtesy of United Artists, Tony Slide, and Walt Disney Productions.

Cover Design by Stefan Dreja

FIRST PUBLISHED 1974
Copyright © 1974 by The Tantivy Press
Library of Congress Catalogue Card No. 73-13190
SBN 0-904208-05-2 (U.K.)
ISBN 0-498-01448-7 (U.S.A.)

Printed in the United States of America

Preface

"The task I'm trying to achieve is above all to make you see."
                                        D. W. GRIFFITH

The films of Howard Hawks, Frank Borzage and Edgar G. Ulmer have little in common. Each director concerns himself with dramatically different levels of experience. In fact, each director's work stands at a different point in a tremendously broad spectrum of theme and style. In a way, their dissimilarities make each film-maker, in the context of this book, a foil for the other, a means of isolating and focusing on the uniqueness of each.

The three essays that follow will attempt not so much to compare or contrast these three artists as to understand how each sees the world through an examination of the form and content of his vision. More than anything else, this book is about visual style. All three directors are storytellers and, like all good storytellers, their tales are inseparable from their telling of them. By looking closely at the way in which each director constructs his films, composes, edits and selects his images, it is possible to see the world as the director himself views it, to understand it through his eyes. This book's goal, like Griffith's, is to make you see.

To the memories of Frank Borzage and Edgar G. Ulmer.

Contents

From the title credits of RIO BRAVO

Howard Hawks

"Whenever I hear a story," says Howard Hawks, "my first thought is how to make it into a comedy, and I think of how to make it into a drama only as a last resort. Do you remember the story about the man who wanted to commit suicide and stayed on the window ledge—*Fourteen Hours*? They wanted me to do it and I said no. 'Why not?' they asked me, 'It's a great story.' I told them that I didn't like suicides, and I told my friend Henry Hathaway that I didn't like the film he had directed. The public didn't like it either, and Zanuck told me I had been right. I told Zanuck: 'I might have done it if it had been Cary Grant getting out of the bedroom of a woman whose husband had come back unexpectedly and after he was found on the ledge, he pretended he was contemplating suicide.' Zanuck asked me if I wanted to start on that one the next day."[*]

Howard Hawks's vision of the world is fundamentally a comic one. Part of his comic sense comes from his brilliant facility for reversing situations and from the innate flexibility and durability of his characters. Despite Pauline Kael's suggestion that Hawks's change of Hildy's sex for *His Girl Friday* (1940) was a logical outgrowth of the newspaper comedy *genre* that developed in the Thirties, this sort of reversal comes naturally for Hawks; this is the way he thinks and similar reversals occur, in one way or another, in almost all his films.[**]

But Hawks's comic vision has deeper roots than the superficial but inherently humorous reversal of roles or plot situations. Hawks tells us that he does not like suicides. His films tell us more: their

[*] Sarris, Andrew, ed., *Interviews with Film Directors*, Bobbs-Merrill Co., Inc., New York, 1967, reprinted by Avon in paper, 1969, p. 237.
[**] *The New Yorker*, February 20, 1971, p. 88.

overall optimism and their assertion of such positive human values as friendship and love deny the possibility of suicide. Hawks's work has a basic humanity that the works of other directors often lack, and it is this humanity that makes his vision comic. In Fritz Lang's films (as often in Bertolt Brecht's plays), there exists a constant tension between the characters and the fatalistic background or world they inhabit. Even when Lang's characters try to express emotion, Lang and his background deny it to them: Lang cuts away in *Human Desire* (1954) from Carl's jealous murder of Owens to an exterior shot of the train on which it is committed. Carl's emotion is equated to and even overshadowed by the mechanistic wheels of fate. Later, Lang obscures Jeff's humane refusal to kill Carl with another train. For Lang, like Claude Chabrol, emotion remains hidden beneath the surface. Even Josef von Sternberg's melodramatic characters who seem to sacrifice all for love, as does Marlene Dietrich as agent X-27 at the end of *Dishonored* (1931), wear impenetrable masks which conceal their real feelings. There is an ironic emptiness in Sternberg characters like Dr. Omar, "the doctor of nothing" in *Shanghai Gesture* (1941), that prevents us from knowing what they feel.

But even in so bleak a Hawks comedy as *I Was a Male War Bride* (1949) with its dark-edged frames and seemingly endless procession of emasculating incidents, there is a resilience to the characters, especially to Cary Grant's Henri Rochard, that allows them to triumph over the dehumanising environment which they inhabit. Although we feel that at any moment Sternberg's fabulous characters could turn into things or become only elaborate extensions of his baroque *décor,* we *know* that neither things, nor backgrounds nor events ever really threaten the humanity of Hawks's characters. We know, even though it is never consciously articulated, that Hawks's characters behave with a sort of inner-directed, self-dictated consistency that precludes their domination by external forces.

The consistency of Hawks's characters grows out of their strong sense of who they are. Their survival depends on an equally strong sense of the physical world around them, a sense of their place in it and how they can adapt themselves to each situation they face and thereby control their world. They are both pragmatic and optimistic; they do the best job they can with the material at hand. In *Rio Bravo,* Pat Wheeler (Ward Bond) asks Chance (John Wayne) how much help he has against the Burdetts. When Chance tells him, Wheeler asks incredulously, "A game-legged old man and a drunk? Is that *all* you've got?" Chance replies, "That's *what* I've got." Chance's re-emphasis epitomises the attitude Hawks's characters take towards whatever problem confronts them. Whether it is Susan (Katharine Hepburn) pretending over the telephone that a leopard is attacking her in order to lure David (Cary Grant) to her in *Bringing Up Baby* (1938) or Cole Thornton (John Wayne), his gun hand paralysed, confronting Nelse McLeod in a shoot-out at the end of *El Dorado* (1966), Hawks's characters face the world head-on, never faltering for a moment or pausing to worry about their limitations. Their adaptability enables them not only to live with the surrounding world, but to use what they have to master it. Their unquestioning committment to the world of positive action reveals Hawks's profound belief that energy and vitality, no matter what the odds, will ensure ultimate triumph.

Hawks roots his films in physical action, shaping his plots around events rather than ideas, and building his characters around concrete gestures and mannerisms rather than abstract inner motivations. We know immediately through the expressiveness of the characters' physical actions how they feel and what they are thinking. They do not need to explain themselves in words; a glance or a gesture communicates more to us than dialogue or an intrusive penetration into their thought processes ever could. At the end of *The Big Sky* (1952), Boone (Dewey Martin) rises and throws an old Blackfoot scalp, taken from the Indian that killed his brother, into the campfire. His movement and his gesture convey his thoughts to us with an immediacy that bypasses any need for their literal articulation. The functional simplicity of Hawks's visual style, which concentrates on actions and refuses to psychoanalyse characters, coupled with the clarity and directness of their actions, creates an intuitive sympathy between Hawks's characters and us. When Boone rises, we *feel* the change that has taken place within him. When he destroys the scalp, we know, without his having spoken a word, that he has come to terms with the hatred that earlier drove him, and that he will return to his Indian wife, Teal Eye. By watching the gestures and movements of Hawks's characters, we understand them as well as they understand one another, and we come to share with them their reactions to events and to each other. Hawks's very physical involvement with his characters and their world makes his films tremendously vivid.

More than any other director, Hawks dwells on the integrity of action, observing it in its wholeness and entirety. He thinks of each action as having a beginning, middle and end and this Aristotelian concept results in an almost compulsive concern for process. In *Scarface* (1932), Gaffney's death in the bowling alley occurs off-screen, suggested symbolically by the strike Gaffney bowls just as he is killed. Hawks's camera follows the bowling ball, showing its source, its progress and its effect. Hawks holds the shot until the last pin falls, implying, in the completeness of the action, the finality of death. In *Tiger Shark* (1932), when Mike (Edward G. Robinson) docks his boat after a successful fishing trip, Hawks shows the crew members at work unloading the fish on conveyor belts. But Hawks then follows the fish down the conveyor belt to the cannery where workers sort and clean Mike's catch. Hawks's concern for the continuity and wholeness of action takes him beyond the point where the work of his central characters stops. He gives the action a life of its own, independent of, yet related indirectly to, his main characters.

The integrity of action offers Hawks's characters an outlet for their inter-personal conflicts and tensions. Since action in a Hawks film has a life of its own, obeying its own rules and following its own processes, characters can, by giving themselves to it, resolve the tensions that develop in their own lives. J. A. Fieschi, in one of the "Cahiers" Hawks issues (January 1963), points out that Hawks tends to alternate scenes of tense character interaction with scenes of impersonal action. The action sequences in *Dawn Patrol* (1930), *Scarface, Only Angels Have Wings* (1939), *Sergeant York* (1941), *Air Force* (1943), *Red River* (1948), *The Big Sky, Land of the Pharaohs* (1955) and *Hatari!* (1962), the fishing sequences in *Tiger Shark*, the racing sequences in *The Crowd Roars* (1932) and *Red Line 7000* (1965), the exterior action sequences in *Rio Bravo,* all have essentially cathartic functions: they serve to relax the tensions between the characters by means of exterior action.

For example, the conflict between Dunson (John Wayne) and Matt (Montgomery Clift) in *Red River* is relaxed by changing the focus of the tensions from interpersonal to impersonal: men cast aside their idiosyncratic differences in order to control the herd. They subordinate their own individuality to a larger identity to achieve their goals. When a character's personality conflicts with the achievement of that goal, as Dunson's ultimately does, the character is seen to have lost sight of his place in the world. Detached from physical reality, he seems to go insane. It is only through impersonal, professional action that characters can maintain their individuality, self-respect and sanity.

In the following pages, I will describe, using a handful of his best films, Hawks's narrative and visual style. Hawks is one of the most difficult directors to analyse. The unobtrusiveness of his visual style and the vitality that brings his characters alive make a serious formal analysis of his work all the harder. Yet, though critical commentary cannot compete with the exciting experience of the films themselves, criticism can enrich that experience. It is the job of the critic here to isolate the elements that make Hawks's films great. This discussion will centre on schematic elements: personal-professional conflicts and the integration of Hawks's characters into their environment.

My affection for Hawks's work makes the analytical restraint which such a study must observe all the more confining. Hopefully, these words will convey a sense of Hawks's greatness and of the pleasure I have drawn from his films.

DAWN PATROL: Courtney (Richard Barthelmess) receives unwelcome orders from Major Brand (Neil Hamilton) in a tense interior sequence

DAWN PATROL and *SCARFACE:*
PERSONALITY VS. PROFESSIONALISM

Dawn Patrol (1930) Hawks's first sound feature, appears, at least initially, severely limited by primitive sound technique: the immobile camera imprisoned within a soundproof glass booth imposes a static look on many of the interior scenes. On closer analysis, however, it becomes quite clear that the film contains a great deal of camera movement—most obviously in the exterior action sequences. Quite naturally, most audiences accept the film in two parts—tense, static, claustrophobic interiors, especially those in the flight commander's office, contrasted with the open, less tense, somewhat fluid, exterior flying sequences. From a pragmatic point of view camera movement could be used out of doors, as when Hawks tracks along the line of planes warming up their engines, because the noise of the engines drowned out camera noise. Also, the sound of action sequences could be post-recorded without split-second synchronisation problems, and insert close-ups could be shot later in the silence of a studio. Nevertheless, despite the practical limitations of early sound film-making, Hawks uses camera mobility and immobility thematically in *Dawn Patrol*. Though perhaps not the innovator of a thematic use of early sound technique, Hawks integrates its limitations into his film quite brilliantly.

The film begins with an aerial dogfight, small planes buzzing each other against the open sky in long shot. Hawks's shooting makes us more aware of the fluidity of motion in a single, spatial continuum (the sky) than of the opposition of the shot's various elements. In other words, we don't know who is who, which planes are Allied, which German. We are only aware of the greater struggle that each plane undergoes to remain aloft during the aerial battle. Though Hawks cuts in to close-up to establish the personality of individual pilots in the planes, the cutting and the camera movement emphasise the overall action and movement of all the planes more than it does any specific Allied-German conflicts. Hawks fades out on the dogfight and fades in on the office of Major Brand (Neil Hamilton). The tensions of this interior setting are immediate and striking. One senses the walls that enclose the characters. Compositional elements, such as the diagonals made by the positioning of Brand's and Phipps's desks, tend to imprison the personalities who inhabit or enter this room. The characters here, especially those who stand at the intersection of these two diagonals—the flight leaders reporting their casualties—are pulled into the composition's static lines. They subordinate their personal feelings to a larger sense of duty.

In contrast to the fluid, confusing action of the film's first scene, there is little movement in the flight commander's office. Characters in it, for the most part, do not move. When they do, Hawks breaks up the force of their movement by cutting on gestures or movement in and out on a single axis. This sort of editing, holding the characters in the same position in the frame, accentuates the taut, impersonal formality of their actions in a restricting environment.

One of the most exciting sequences in *Dawn Patrol* occurs at the moment when the stasis of responsibility and kinesis of personal feeling come into direct conflict—the scene between Scott (Douglas Fairbanks Jr.) and Courtney (Richard Barthelmess) after the death of Scott's younger brother. Hawks shoots Scott's entrance into the bar-room adjoining the flight commander's office with a tracking close-up of Scott's feet. The shot gives Scott's movement a great deal of emotional force. As Scott enters Court's office and approaches him, the camera, which until this time has hardly ever moved in this room, tracks in on both men. The track-in suggests a dramatic breakthrough of feeling in a static environment in which emotion has always been sacrificed to professional necessity. In a sense it works as a violation of the room's mood and marks a deepening of the tension between the characters and the roles they must perform to survive.

The structure of the film leads towards a resolution of this tension. By alternating fluid, exterior scenes with static interior ones, Hawks creates two distinct, almost antithetical moods and establishes something like a convulsive pattern or rhythm between interior and exterior sequences. We begin to anticipate the release of tensions in exterior action sequences at the point of highest emotional tension in the interiors. For this reason, Courtney's final flight, in which he sacrifices himself for his friend Scott and also atones for the death of Scott's younger brother (note the insert shot of the boy's crew medal in Court's plane just before the final dogfight), is cathartic: the explosions caused by his bombing of the munitions dump—action more damaging and destructive than any previous mission—correspond to an explosion within Courtney. It releases tensions and resolves the action with a completeness rivalled only by the dynamiting of the Burdett's warehouse at the end of *Rio Bravo*.

The film's overall structure develops a pattern of inevitability. Each character becomes trapped between the inevitability of his situation and his own personal feelings. The static tension that ensues from this professional-vs.-personal conflict is tremendously debilitating in each case. After Brand's departure, we see Courtney sitting in the same position, performing similar actions—answering the telephone and carrying out its impersonal orders—and using similar gestures. He is trapped into becoming like Brand by performing Brand's role, just as Scott later becomes somewhat like the earlier Courtney (and Brand) when he gives orders to the men. In one repeated scene, the flight commander (first Brand, then Court and finally Scott) enters the bar-room to issue the day's orders. Hawks shoots these nearly identical scenes very formally, with dark foreground figures rigidly looking at and listening to the flight commander in the background, and repeats the same set-up with each successive flight commander. Everything looks the same. Only the flight commander and the names on the flight list in the background have changed.

Like the relationship between Scott and Courtney, that between Lt. Michel Denet (Fredric March) and Capt. Paul Laroche (Warner Baxter) in *The Road to Glory* (1936), set in the grim context of trench warfare, also reveals a personal-professional conflict. Though in each case the men have personal dissimilarities, the responsibility of their positions forces them into a strained singleness of identity as division commanders.

The constant threat of death that surrounds each character forces him to subordinate his personal will to the larger, impersonal necessity that the war creates. As a result, Hawks's soldiers, like his pilots in *Dawn Patrol,* fight not so much a literal enemy as a weakness within themselves. When Denet hears the moans of a wounded soldier entangled in barbed-wire in no-man's land, he gives one of his men permission to go out after him; yet Denet's action results only in another casualty. The off-screen cries continue until Laroche, as he must, shoots the wounded man to keep his men from dying in the attempt to save him.

The only outlet for the tension resulting from friction between characters and the roles they must perform in these action films is the action itself. At the end of *Road to Glory*, Laroche, now blind, and his father, who earlier disgraced himself in combat, sacrifice themselves in a suicide mission. In *Dawn Patrol,* characters lose their individuality in the action sequences by becoming one with their planes. It is only by submitting their individuality to a larger action that Hawks's characters can redeem themselves. The best example of this occurs when Courtney takes off on his final, one-way flight behind enemy lines. The take-off is shot with only one cut, showing the face of Court's mechanic after take-off, and without camera movement. As the plane flies farther and farther away from the camera, we become less and less aware of Courtney and more and more aware of the plane. Courtney *becomes* the plane.

In the flight commander's office, professionalism is static and full of tensions; in the air, it is fluid and mobile. In both spheres it tends to rob characters of their uniqueness, to make them impersonal parts of a machine. In the flight commander's office, characters resist this, and the result is tension. In the air, the pilots give themselves willingly over to their mission and resolve their tensions through cathartic action.

In comparison with a film like *Dawn Patrol*, constructed around the alternation of long, static sequences with seemingly shorter, kinetic, action scenes, *Scarface* (1932) bustles with continuous motion. The first scene, shot in a single take, is built around a long, tracking shot and the movement of characters in and out of the frame; it consists of continuous action within a single temporal unit. The action of the rest of the film remains remarkably dynamic. Even the film's episodic structure contributes to its fluidity; the background locations and characters constantly change; only the major characters standing in front of them remain the same. Things happen so quickly in *Scarface* that Hawks rarely has the opportunity to develop a feeling of stasis in a locale or set as he does in *Dawn Patrol*; he only infrequently cuts back to a camera set-up that has been used before.

If lack of camera movement in *Dawn Patrol* helps to express its characters' imprisonment in professional roles, the presence of character and camera movement in *Scarface* is an almost nightmarish inversion of that: constant change prevents the characters from establishing themselves with any stability in their universe. Every action in the film adheres to a rigid pattern; though the universe changes constantly, it changes in a predictable, almost inevitable way. Once Louis Costillo, the first gangster boss, gets what he wants and sits "on top of the world," he falls and is replaced by another gangster just like him, first Lovo then Tony Camonte (Paul Muni). Every movement and change in *Scarface* contains the seeds of its own doom and pushes the characters towards their own destruction.

Hawks sets his personalities against a background of events that inexorably shift the characters towards powerlessness and paralysis. One murder leads to another, and the repetition of murders, like the use of crosses to mark each one, sets up a pattern of expectation that cannot be frustrated. Like a composer of music, Hawks varies this repetition of a single theme, finally turning it upon itself: the killer is killed. Each murder drives another nail into Camonte's own coffin as he further implicates himself in the film's inevitable pattern of events.

Against the background of this impersonal action that exists almost independently of the characters is set Tony Camonte's flamboyant personality, animating the film's deadeningly mechanical action. His likeable vitality and boundless energy work against the impersonal events and actions he performs. Tony's idiosyncratic behaviour creates a tension between his professional and personal identity that tragically erupts near the end of the film when, crazed by his possessive quasi-incestuous relationship with his sister, Cesca (Ann Dvorak), Tony kills Rinaldo (George Raft), a loyal friend and follower, who has secretly married her.

Tony does not struggle against the pattern of events that leads to his own death. At times, he seems unaware of it. Yet, like Costillo and Lovo, his rise implies his eventual fall, and each additional trapping of success—new suits, shirts, a bullet-proof car, Lovo's former girlfriend Poppy—entangles him further in the course of events that destroys him.

Opposite: Tony Camonte (Paul Muni) reprimands his sister Cesca (Ann Dvorak), for going out with men, in SCARFACE

Similarly, in *The Big Sleep* (1946), detective Philip Marlowe (Humphrey Bogart) is swept along by a series of incidents he can neither understand nor control. The episodic nature of this later film, the endless stream of minor characters and subplots and the impenetrable, complex, Faulknerian story, force Marlowe into a passive relationship with his environment. Only when Marlowe begins actively to resist the events that catch him up in their flow, does he regain control over them. In one remarkable scene, Marlowe, beaten and bound by thugs, sits powerless on the floor in the centre of the frame. Taking command of the situation, he persuades Vivian (Lauren Bacall) to move a lamp that is shining in his eyes, to pour him a drink and light him a cigarette and finally to cut him loose. Though physically powerless, he dominates the scene. Later, manipulating the action for the first time in the film, Marlowe arranges a showdown with Eddie Mars, sets a trap for him and, in a cathartic outburst of brutality, shoots to maim Mars, forcing his enemy into an ambush set for himself as Cole Thornton does to his enemies in *El Dorado*.

In *The Big Sleep*, Marlowe eventually establishes control of the events around him; in *Scarface*, Tony Camonte remains their slave. After he kills Rinaldo, he never regains power over his world. He is victimised by the pattern of events he himself initiated. At the opening of the film, Hawks's introduction of Tony as a dark shadow on the wall de-personalises his murder of Costillo, transforming it into a kind of ritual. The circular camera movement that tracks in from the street to meet the action and pans out with its completion re-inforces the treatment of the event as part of a larger cycle of action unknown to and independent of the specific characters involved in it. During the killing, Tony acts mechanically. Even the seemingly idiosyncratic whistling of an aria from "Lucia di Lammermoor" turns out to be a rite Tony observes whenever he commits murder. In fact, later, when he and Gino murder Lovo, Lovo pleads with them for his life, only to face their cold, mechanical gestures: Gino calmly flips his habitual coin and Tony, whistling his aria, turns and puts his fist through Lovo's name on his office door, changing it just as he had earlier changed the name on Costillo's door.

The repetition of action in this film gives the events a nightmarish life of their own and a power so overwhelming that characters must surrender to it. Characters remain paralysed by events and, as if on a ferris wheel, are carried back to where they started. Like the revolving beacon which opens *Ceiling Zero* (1936) and suggests the ritualistic routine that follows, the street light that goes off at the start of the film is reflected at the film's conclusion by the "Cook's Tours" sign that blinks on and off above Tony Camonte, dead in the gutter.

THE BIG SLEEP: Marlowe (Humphrey Bogart) helps Vivian (Lauren Bacall) outwit a would-be robber

TWENTIETH CENTURY and HIS GIRL FRIDAY: THE HAR-MONY OF PERSONALITY AND PROFESSION

The drama in *Dawn Patrol* arises from the conflict between the characters and their environment, between their own personalities and the roles their job forces them to play. Hawks's comedies resolve this conflict between characters and events, emphasising a more flexible harmony of personality and action. The inflexible nature of Hawks's characters in adventure films like *Dawn Patrol, Scarface, Tiger Shark, Viva Villa* (1934) etc., doggedly leads them to their own destruction. But in the comedies, characters yield to the changing world around them, thereby preserving themselves in it, like trees bending in a strong wind. By giving themselves wholly to the world around them, they achieve mastery over it and obtain what they want. Often Hawks shows this process through a loss of identity. Each alteration in the environment brings on a corresponding change of personality in Hawks's chameleon-like characters, enabling them to endure, to deal with and to control the world-in-flux around them.

Twentieth Century (1934) deals explicitly with actors and reveals more clearly than perhaps any other Hawks comedy how characters can control their environment by playing the roles it thrusts upon them. The opening rehearsal sequence initiates both Mildred Plotke (Carole Lombard) and us into the world of the theatre, a world in which real emotion is channelled into stage melodramatics. Plotke's transformation into Lily Garland at the hands of producer-director Oscar Jaffe (John Barrymore) marks the loss of a superficial identity but brings with it the realisation of a new identity as actress that goes beyond the dull caricatured existence and limited expressiveness of Mildred Plotke, the shopgirl. At the start of rehearsals, Jaffe beckons her over with his finger and, in an hypnotically tender, fatherly voice, explains her part to her: "Now don't be nervous child. You're not Lily Garland anymore. You're little Mary Jo Calhoun . . ." Later, reversing his earlier tenderness, Jaffe pushes and bullies Lily into an emotional break-down, uncovering an expressiveness he could find by no other means. The sorrows of life, he tells her, become the joys of art: to teach Lily to scream, he pricks her with a pin. Her real cry of pain becomes a stage cry, directed and produced by Jaffe. A wipe by Hawks turns Jaffe's and Oliver Webb's hand-clapping into the applause of the opening-night audience after Lily's successful *début*. Her transformation into an actress concludes with a shot of a newly-hung star on Lily's dressing-room door.

Once Lily becomes an actress, her relationship with Oscar, both professional and personal, is more volatile, filled with over-theatrical partings and reconciliations; yet their reactions to one another convey the underlying durability of their partnership and the rightness of their union: their affectedly dramatic temperaments suit them perfectly to one another. Oscar's strange hold over Lily, a comic parody by Barrymore of his famous role in *Svengali* (1931), rests on his ability to out-act her, to take better advantage of situations and events, manipulating them to win her back again and again. Midway through the film, the action shifts to the Chicago-to-New York Twentieth Century Limited. The enclosed world of the train, hurtling through space, has it own rules, rules that Jaffe quickly learns to manipulate. Like his lightning-fast changes of mood and flexible adoption of various postures, Jaffe's rapid adjustment to the train's world reflects his responsiveness to the changing demands of each situation he finds himself in. Trying to sign an unwilling Lily to another contract before they reach New York, Oscar transforms the train into a theatre and each compartment into a separate stage for another "Jaffe Production." Faking a broken arm (to which he repeatedly points) to ensure his safety, Jaffe badgers Lily's society boy-friend into playing the part of a jealous lover in his impromptu melodrama. When he gets the lover to leave Lily's compartment, Oscar remarks, "What an exit! Not a word. That's what we should have done when Michael exits at the end of the first act in 'The Heart of Kentucky'!"

Twentieth Century ends with a theatrical masterstroke. During another of Jaffe's fake suicide attempts, his friends, tired of "the old Dutch act," walk out on him. A harmlessly insane religious fanatic enters, takes Jaffe's gun and accidentally shoots him. Jaffe quickly recovers from his melodramatics over the minor flesh wound, and has an idea. Rearranging furniture and lights in the parlour car, he places himself in centre stage and contrives an elaborate death scene to make Lily sign his contract as a last request. Told of Oscar's imminent demise, Lily grabs a scarf (even in supposedly "real" situations, Lily uses props to help express her feelings) and rushes to Jaffe's side. Reacting more to the emotional effectiveness of Jaffe's scene than to its credibility, Lily signs the contract.

The final scene, a rehearsal of Jaffe's next play, takes us back to the film's first scene. Repeating his original speech and theatrical gestures, Jaffe, tyrannical as ever with Lily, finds fault with her performance, demands a piece of chalk and starts to sketch out her movements, as he had when she was a novice, and forces her to obey exactly his orders.

Jaffe's tremendous strength, supplying life to the characters around him, makes him the dramatic centre of the film. His inexhaustible endurance, his refusal to give up however bad things get, lend positive value to his schemes, Protean theatrics and Machiavellian manipulations of other characters. An actor, Jaffe realises his potentialities best when acting a part. If nothing else, his acting vindicates itself by getting him what he wants. Though he never says it in so many words, he loves Lily and she loves him. His devious attempts to win her back reflect the depth of his feeling for her, just as her resistance to these attempts reflects her feeling. "In some Humpty Dumpty way that was true love," comments Owen, Jaffe's friend and press agent. Lily's willingness to go back to Jaffe again and again reveals her recognition of his vitality and of her need for him. Jaffe's total integration into the theatre does not rob him of his own individuality; it helps him to realise it, providing him with a form through which he can express himself. Jaffe gives himself whole-heartedly to his profession, gains strength from it and maintains his uniqueness through it. His engagement with the world around him creates a unity of character and action that remains a trademark of Hawks comedy.

In Hawks's films, characters define themselves by their relationship to their environment: not only each character's narrative background, i.e. his profession, but also his iconographic environment, the composition of each frame, the surrounding characters and objects to which Hawks's central characters relate. Their ability to control their environment determines just how "good" they are at their profession and just how well they integrate themselves into the world around them.

His Girl Friday (1940), like *Twentieth Century,* deals with this process; it depicts one character's integration and reintegration into a profession through another character's manoeuvring of people and events. The re-engagement of Hildy Johnson (Rosalind Russell) with her environment and with its agent, Walter Burns (Cary Grant), goes beyond personal conflict as it appears in *Twentieth Century* to solve the problem that Hildy's need for professionalism and her conflicting pursuit of personal happiness create.

Robin Wood faults *His Girl Friday* because the choice Hawks offers Hildy between a home in Albany with Bruce Baldwin (Ralph Bellamy) and a return to the newspaper business with Walter Burns "is much too narrow to be acceptable."* Hawks, however,

* Wood, Robin, "Howard Hawks," Doubleday & Co., Inc., New York; Secker and Warburg, London, 1968, p. 77.

never really offers Hildy a choice. From the moment she enters the paper's newsroom and walks through it to Walter's office, she is powerless to reverse the process that her appearance there sets in motion. The foreground and background engage her as she reacts to and greets her old friends in the office, situating her with an irrevocable finality in that environment. *His Girl Friday* presents definition of character through physical setting and an inexorability of events that sweep characters along in their flow. Seen in these terms, Hildy's return to her profession and to Walter becomes inevitable. The only real issues left in question are how and when Walter will win her back and how and when she will discover that the only resolution of her personal and professional conflicts lies in remarrying her editor-in-chief.

Walter's greatest strengths lie in his sureness of himself and of Hildy, and in his ability to manipulate events. His power is quite physical. Like a player in a game of squash, Walter positions himself in the frame where he can best handle whatever comes his way. At the restaurant, he grabs Bruce's chair, placing himself between Bruce and Hildy. This position enables him to dominate Hildy physically: he borrows her match to light his own cigarette. His cynical remarks about Albany and Bruce's profession elicit physical responses from her. And by kicking his leg to shut him up, Hildy reveals a greater physical intimacy with Walter than with Bruce.

Later, Hawks replaces Walter, physically absent from the press-room at the criminal courts building, with a series of events which, by re-awakening Hildy's professionalism, draw her away from Bruce and bring her closer to Walter. Just as Hildy is about to leave the pressroom and rejoin Bruce, Earl Williams, the harmless but insane victim of "production for use," escapes. As the other reporters call in the news, Hawks cuts rapidly to brief close-ups of each, capturing the excitement and immediacy of the moment. The quickness of the cutting treats the newsmen not as individuals but as fast-working, efficient professionals doing their job. As the reporters rush out leaving Hildy standing alone in the room, the newspaperman in her responds to the demands of the moment. Caught up in the excitement of the event and in the frenetic pace of the other reporters, she takes off her hat and coat, phones Burns, dashes out and brings back a scoop on the escape.

Later, when she captures Earl Williams and hides him in a desk in the pressroom, Walter joins her there and re-establishes his physical control over her. Thinking her job finished, Hildy again tries to leave to find Bruce (whom Walter has safely tucked away in jail) and take the train with him to Albany. Walter, however, starts telling her how important it is for her to stay and write up her story exposing the city's political corruption. His rapidly delivered monologue quickens the tempo of the action; his gestures and movements dominate the frame. Backing her around the room, Walter takes physical charge of her and the room, controlling not only the pace of the action but the action itself. Hildy, unable to resist Walter's harangue, finally abandons herself to the event, sits down and begins typing her story. While she is typing and Walter is rearranging the front page by telephone, Bruce enters and tries to interrupt them. He stands helpless and ignored in the background, excluded from the professional action in the foreground. All Bruce can do is repeat to Hildy that he's taking the next train to Albany. But Hildy, totally absorbed in what she's doing, doesn't hear him. Defeated by Walter and the newspaper profession, Bruce walks out.

Walter's victory over Bruce arises from his tremendous energy and his refusal to yield so much as an inch of ground to his opponent in the battle for Hildy. At the same time, Walter shrewdly uses Hildy's professionalism to lure her away from Bruce. Like Jaffe, Walter declares his love for her through his scheming to keep her as his star reporter. At the end of the film, when Walter "nobly" sends her after Bruce, Hildy breaks into tears thinking that Walter doesn't love her anymore because he no longer schemes to keep her. But she is unaware that Walter's trickery has again put Bruce out of her reach in jail and that Walter's "noble" action is really a final proof of his love.

Though Ben Hecht and Charles MacArthur set out to express their contempt for journalism in writing "The Front Page," their play became, in their own words, "a Valentine thrown to the past." The film retains much of the stage play's original cynicism and bitterness but little of its nostalgic sentiment. Hawks translates Hecht and MacArthur's fondness for their central characters into a respect for their mastery of their profession, undermining, to some degree, the authors' more critical attitudes. The Earl Williams story remains in the background, shut away in the desk with Williams himself, and functioning more as an event through which Walter and Hildy are reunited than as a moral issue that might force us to question their actions. Though elements in the script condemn journalists and their Machiavellian outlook, Hawks builds his film more around the positive strength of his characters' pursuit of their goals than around the questionable value of the goals themselves.

The comic tone of *His Girl Friday*, governed more by the limitless energy and endurance of Walter and Hildy than by the passive submissiveness of Bruce and Earl, enables us to share Hawks's admiration and respect for Walter's and Hildy's professional control of the action, and immunises us against the film's more serious elements. Hildy's rejection of the lifeless security offered her by Bruce in favour of Walter's lively insecurity, emerges in the context of the film as an affirmation of Walter's greatest strengths, his endurance and flexibility. Hawks's unswerving fidelity to consistency of tone and character commits him and us to an acknowledgement of the rightness of the reunion of Walter and Hildy and a recognition of the physical effect their environment has on them. Though the film's final gag—Hildy follows Walter out of the pressroom carrying her own suitcase—has a double-edge, it is more triumphant than tragic. It marks Hildy's final acceptance of the identity her profession and her environment have given her.

ONLY ANGELS HAVE WINGS

Only Angels Have Wings (1939) is Hawks's first real masterpiece. It is characterised by an economical, eloquent visual style that understates dramatic situations and deeply emotional bonds of loyalty, friendship and love; and a narrative density that simultaneously develops the actions and stories of several pairs of interdependent characters. With the exception of *Rio Bravo,* it is Hawks's most compact film. At times, it treats a whole range of feelings, shared by a number of characters, in a single gesture and, through this gesture, ties all the characters together into an organic unit. When Joe Souther (Noah Beery, Jr.) ascends into the thick fog, threading his plane through the tall mountains surrounding the airstrip, Geoff Carter (Cary Grant) and Bonnie Lee (Jean Arthur) both let out their breath at the same time, releasing the anxiety they feel over Joe's dangerous take-off. This shared gesture, subtle yet revealing, binds Geoff and Bonnie together, establishing a relationship between them by making them partners in a single experience.

Script, even more than gesture, contributes to the film's density. On one level, the circular story structure compounds the intensity of action through repetition. For example, when the Kid (Thomas Mitchell) dies, the experience is intensified for us by the fact that it echoes the death of Joe Souther earlier in the film. And we know without being told that the arrival of the mail boat at the end, shot the same way it was at the beginning, signals both the professional demands of Geoff's job—its load of mail must be flown out—and their personal counterpart—Bonnie Lee is to leave on the same boat.

On another level, the dialogue's obliqueness repeatedly underplays characters' feelings, and this paradoxically intensifies them. After Joe's death, all Geoff can say is, "Got a match?" Yet his reading of the line conveys his inner anguish. Later, when the Kid dies, Geoff looks at his friend's possessions and remarks, "Not much to show for twenty-two . . ." but breaks off in mid-sentence and rushes out, trying to suppress his grief.

Thematically, *Only Angels Have Wings* deals with integration: the integration of Bat (Richard Barthelmess) and of Bonnie Lee into the group become two of the film's central concerns. But though it may not appear obvious at first, the film is also about the integration of Geoff. Throughout the film Geoff attempts to conceal and to control his feelings. This attempt produces one of the film's most significant sequences: Bonnie Lee comes into his office to say good-bye and finds Geoff crying over the Kid's death, surrendering himself totally to a sentiment to which he was previously invulnerable. Geoff's sorrow, felt in his silence and seen in his moist eyes, strips away his earlier strength and solidity, establishing a moment of genuine, profoundly moving tenderness between him and Bonnie. But Hawks refuses to let Geoff indulge his feelings. Tex's voice on the radio announces that the mountain pass is clear and the news, restoring Geoff's professional self-control, sets in motion a flurry of activity. Much as the sudden, emergency take-off of the aeroplane Mary Ann in *Air Force* compels Sgt. White (Harry Carey) to suppress his grief over his son's death, the immediacy of Geoff's job forces into the background his regret and sadness over the Kid's death. Professionalism draws Geoff back to reality, providing an outlet for his grief in action. In the last few shots of the film Geoff and Les, both wounded, fly off with the mail, dependent on one another to get the job done.

Gestures in the film reflect the growth of this process of integration and interdependence. Bat's gestures, for instance, are self-contained and isolate him from the rest of the group. He does not touch other characters or reach out willingly to them. His handshake comes reluctantly when he is first introduced to the other fliers. In Geoff's office, his gestures are similarly self-contained; he fidgets with his hat band and spins the propeller blade of a model plane on the desk while Geoff talks to Hartwood on the phone. Though Bat's gestures on the ground are tense and uneasy, his first flight dissolves all that, making his professional competence a means both of self-expression and of redemption. In one continuous aerial shot, his plane, seen against a dizzyingly changing background, circles a small plateau in the Andes and drops towards it, landing on a dangerously short strip. The overwhelming presence of nature in the surrounding mountains, cliffs and valleys makes Bat's control of his plane all the more marvellous. Bat's ability to do his job well releases him from the tensions that accompany him on the ground.

The final scene with Bat in the bar—his two hands burned and bandaged—pulls him out of the isolation he feels when he is on the ground. The fliers make an attempt to bring Bat into their group: the Kid, a former enemy now dead, "buys" him a drink, Les puts the drink into his bandaged hands, Pancho gives him a cigarette, and Geoff holds Bat's cigarette while he drinks. Though Bat's gestures are still essentially self-contained (because his hands are burned, he can't use them), the other characters—some, like Les and Geoff, wounded themselves—draw Bat into their group.

Part of Bat's integration is accomplished through behaviour. It is also reinforced by Hawks's composition, which physically defines the group by setting the fliers off from the characters who surround them. Thus Gent, who stands at the bar in the background and who has become an outsider because he was not good enough—he was afraid to fly a cargo of nitroglycerine—becomes a defining force within the frame: his health emphasises the fliers' injuries that they sustained while doing their job. It is partially the presence of Gent, who was not good enough, that integrates Bat into the group of fliers who *are* good enough and who have the injuries to prove it.

Throughout the film, Hawks uses background characters to define the foreground action. This is done in such a non-obtrusive way that one is rarely aware of the process. The initial antagonism between Bat and the fliers, especially since it is worked into the script, is fairly obvious. However, what Hawks does visually with Bonnie Lee, a somewhat similarly intrusive figure, is much more subtle. Like Gent, Bonnie is also seen in the background of the frame (although only in the middle of the film). The best instance of this occurs when Bat and the two girls, Felicia and Elena, arrive on a boat. When Geoff enters the bar to meet Bat, he passes Bonnie and leaves her standing in the back of the frame. When he greets the two girls who, like Bonnie, have come in on the boat and whom Geoff has known in the past, it is possible to see Bonnie in the background.

Though the emphasis of the scene remains on the identification of Bat, on seeing through the confusion of names and faces, Bonnie's presence in the frame adds another dimension to the action. She sees here, as she does later when she spies on Judy (Rita Hayworth) and Geoff, her future. She could become another Felicia. Or another Judy. Her presence in the background not only shows her exclusion from the group, it also clarifies her relationship with Geoff. Hawks only re-integrates her at the end of the film. When Geoff gives her the Kid's coin, she takes the Kid's place, inheriting his intimacy with Geoff and his position in the group.

Hawks's framing and treatment of space helps his actors define themselves. Groups in Hawks, clearly, are not only welded together on a narrative level by a common goal or danger but also on a compositional level by those outsiders who do not share those goals

AIR FORCE: Winocki (John Garfield) avenges the death of one of his comrades

or dangers. Major Brand in *Dawn Patrol*, for instance, operates as a defining figure: his exclusion from the group of pilots defines that group.

Hawks's use of composition to set up conflicts within the frame and to specify the relationships among his characters reflects, on a visual level, his interest in the integration of his characters with one another and with their environment. When they are totally absorbed into a group or environment—when they have subordinated

35

their own desires, idiosyncracies and needs to the larger needs of the group—Hawks tends to show them (though this is completely unschematic and intuitive on his part) in two-dimensional space, bound together in a single spatial continuum. When his characters' conflict with their environment or one another stands unresolved, Hawks suggests this visually in more or less three-dimensional shots. In *Air Force,* for instance, Hawks alternates two-dimensional shots of the plane in the air (in which the men *become* the plane) with three-dimensional shots of the plane landing or taking off amid smoke, damaged hangars, trees, etc. (conflict between the plane and its environment). All of Hawks's films, by alternating three-dimensional, personal, idiosyncratic footage with two-dimensional, *im*personal action footage, work towards the goal of total integration in two dimensions.

RED RIVER

Many critics of *Red River* (1948)—even Borden Chase who wrote its screenplay—argue that Hawks's ending is absurdly inconsistent with the rest of the film.° Yet the ending is one of the most perfect in all cinema; it has a beauty, logic and integrity that is consistent both with what has gone before and with the positive qualities of Hawks's comic perception of man's relationship to other men and to his environment. Because the consistency of characters and characters' relationships is more important to Hawks than plot consistency in *Red River,* we know that Dunson (John Wayne) and Matt (Montgomery Clift) will never kill one another. It is clear from the way Matt repeatedly gives Dunson his own cigarette, from the way Matt naturally and automatically joins with Dunson in shooting his enemies—Don Diego's man, Bunk, and the three "quitters"—and from the intensity of Matt's reaction when Tyler wants to shoot

___
° "Film Comment," Vol. 6, No. 4, Winter 1970–71, pp. 15–16.

RED RIVER: the first shot, with its diagonal movement from right to left. Historical sweep shown in long shot, personal story in close-up

Dunson, that there is a physical bond between the two men that the mechanics of Borden Chase's story cannot break. It is Hawks's assertion of the intuitive, human responses between Matt and Dunson that makes *Red River* comic rather than tragic. The greatness of Hawks's ending resides in its overwhelming commitment to physical reality and its total rejection of conventional form; in its adherence to consistency of characterisation and in its inspired frustration of the rigid demands of traditional dramatic expectation.

One of the greatest qualities of *Red River* is its epic scope. It is an expansive film, covering a long interval of time, dealing with a large number of characters and an enormous herd of cattle, and stretching across a vast geographical area. The stature of its characters depends, in large part, on this scope—on their ability to control such a herd, their determination to cross such a space and achieve what seems impossible. Naturally, the background in the film figures quite importantly in the treatment of characters and the development of the story. At the risk of simplifying Hawks's complex and subtle visual style, I'd like to point out an image that recurs throughout the film and that suggests the breadth of the film's scope and its timelessness. This image (of diagonal movement) first appears in the opening shots of the film: a train of covered wagons moves diagonally, from right to left, through the

RED RIVER: the herd moves diagonally from right to left

frame and one wagon, Dunson's, pulls out of the train. The continual movement of wagons in the background throughout the first scene has a powerful emotional effect. When Dunson's wagon finally pulls away, at right angles, from this line, the movement of wagons in two directions out of the frame heightens our sense of Fen's isolation in the centre of the composition. When Hawks cuts back to a final medium shot of Fen, the wagons moving in the background seem to draw her away from Dunson. At the same time, the seemingly eternal movement easily bridges the fourteen years that occur between this shot and the one that takes its place in our minds a few scenes later—the shot of Dunson, Matt and Groot (Walter Brennan) talking about the cattle drive as the herd moves, from right to left, in the distance. The background of *Red River*, especially during the drive, is constantly in motion. But unlike the similarly fluid but distinctly chaotic background and motion in the exterior scenes of *Male War Bride*, the background of *Red River* seems to move in one direction only. It is this "direction" of the background movement that offers not only physical continuity from scene to scene but also a non-specific sense of an inevitable destination. Hawks repeats this image again and again, setting a more or less static foreground figure or group of figures against a moving background. For instance, the shot of Matt and the herd deserting Dunson while Dunson leans on his horse watching them recalls the similar image of Fen and the wagons. This type of image repetition works unconsciously throughout the film to tie one specific moment to another in a timeless way that unifies these scenes.

Hawks augments the epic dimension of his images with a similarly patterned narrative. The plot, constructed like a musical theme and variations, consists mostly of journeys to specific destinations, e.g. Dunson and Groot reach the Red River; Dunson, along with Matt and Groot, finds a site for his future ranch; Dunson and his men drive the herd to Abilene. Hawks follows each arrival at a destination, landmark or goal with an outburst of action, a fight or an event that releases tensions built up over the journey: at the Red River Hawks shows Dunson's first fight-encounter with Matt; at the ranch-site we see his shoot-out with Don Diego's men; in Abilene Hawks presents a final gun- and fist-fight. Throughout the long drive, the journey of each day seems to conclude with some minor or major· conflict around the campfire. Together with this development of a journey-conflict *motif,* Hawks alternates impersonal, man-vs.-nature struggles (long shots of men trying to control the herd by day) with interpersonal, man to man clashes (medium and close shots of men and their disputes at night). Hawks's repetition and alternation of journey and conflict, of impersonal and interpersonal elements, of day and night, contribute to the film's overpowering epic momentum.

The visual style of *Red River* is built on static set-ups: shots of movement through the frames. The crossing of the Red River is a good example: most of the shots of the herd are static with the exception of a few short pans. But when the camera does move, as it does in the shot from Groot's wagon, its effect is quite powerful. Like the first tracking shot in *Hatari!,* this movement engages us directly with the action. But the reverse-tracking shots of Dunson with his hired guns riding after Matt, and those of his final walk through the herd to face Matt, disengage us from Dunson. Movement towards the camera in Hawks's films has always been somewhat threatening. The direct movement of Mike's face into the camera at the end of *Tiger Shark* is full of menace. The reverse-tracks in *Red River* seem threatening because they violate the film's overall pattern of oblique movement, from right to left, through the frame. Even the 180-degree pan which begins the cattle drive, though it has depth at specific moments, appears, on the whole, to be flat; the backgrounds seem contained. But at the end of the film, it is almost as though the patterned movement that has run throughout the backgrounds. can no longer be contained. Once the men complete the cattle drive, and the milling cattle, settled in the streets of Abilene, no longer provide background movement, individual character motion becomes independent of the background. The shot of Dunson walking through the herd suggests not merely danger, but, in the context of the film's other movements, insanity. At certain points in the film, specific backgrounds seem to hold the characters in check—thus, the three-shot of Dunson, Matt and Groot is balanced by the graves of the men who tried to take the place away from Dunson. What is initially so terrifying about the final scene is Dunson's apparent escape from the hold of his background: he moves through the cattle and crosses the railroad tracks

RED RIVER: Fen (Coleen Gray) and Dunson (John Wayne). Frame enlargement

without seeming to be affected by them. The awesomeness of Dunson's walk comes from its unstoppable momentum, reflecting Dunson's stubborn determination to dominate the world around him. It is only when Dunson meets resistance—when Matt fights back and the two crash comically into a wagonful of pots and pans—that their fight can stop. It is only the intervention of a character who emerges from that background, namely Tess (Joanne Dru), that brings a restoration of sanity and order.

The chaotic comedy of *Red River*'s ending contrasts dramatically with the orderly seriousness of the film's first sequence; yet it develops logically and naturally out of the first scene and it works as a final resolution of conflicts. *Red River* begins impersonally: shots of a book entitled "Tales of Texas" dissolve into a long shot of a wagon train. When Dunson's more personal story begins, as his wagon pulls out of the train, Hawks cuts in to medium shots. Finally, when Dunson kisses Fen good-bye, Hawks cuts in to a powerful close-up. Alternating the impersonal sweep of history with personal and idiosyncratic instants, Hawks cuts, throughout the film, from long to medium shot, using the close-up at only the most intimate moments.

Describing the double vision of John Ford's *Stagecoach* (1939), Andrew Sarris writes that, "what makes Ford's characters unique in the Western Epic is their double image, alternating between close-ups of emotional intimacy and long shots of epical involvement, thus capturing both the twitches of life and the silhouettes of legend."* In *Red River*, Hawks tends to set historical patterns of inevitability in long shot against personal idiosyncrasies in close-up. Dunson's sacrifice of personal happiness (Fen) to some larger, less personal goal (his ranch and the herd) epitomises the film's overall

---

* "*Stagecoach* in 1939 and in Retrospect," "Action," Sept.–Oct. 1971, p. 33.

RED RIVER: Fen watches Dunson set out on his own. Frame enlargement

conflict between the personal and the impersonal. What makes *Red River* a comedy and what makes Hawks different from Ford is the quality of the film's montage. Where Ford's long shot/close-up editing idealises his characters, the same sort of cutting in Hawks's films humanises his. Where Ford is more apt to end a long shot/close-up sequence in long shot, Hawks is more likely to end it in close-up. If Hawks had ended *Only Angels Have Wings* with a medium-long shot of Geoff and Les's plane taking off rather than with the close-up of Bonnie Lee (with which it *does* end), the tone of the last sequence and of the picture as a whole would have changed from one of triumph to one of loss. Similarly, the close-up editing at the end of *Red River* releases the film's characters from

43

the epic patterns of inevitability that formerly isolated them from one another and restores their sense of themselves and of their place in their environment. Hawks's decision to break down the film's inevitable momentum in this last scene and to end the film in a close-up is deliberate and reaffirms the overwhelming strength and persistence of his comic vision.

RIO BRAVO

Hawks's films scripted by Jules Furthman, *Only Angels Have Wings, To Have and Have Not* (1944) and *Rio Bravo* (1959), sustain several stories in a single, structural matrix of nearly simultaneous events that feed into and off of one another, creating a self-sufficient, self-contained organic unit. Unlike more temporally disjointed films, such as *Sergeant York, Red River, The Big Sky, El Dorado* or *Rio Lobo* (1970), *Rio Bravo* distills its action into a time span of a few days. Everything seems to happen at once. In *Red River*, discreet actions and images recur successively, giving the film a paratactic structure. In *Rio Bravo*, actions, relationships and images occur hypotactically: rather than being spread out in time, as in *Red River*, they seem to happen on top of one another. Seen in the context of *Red River's* epic expansiveness, *Rio Bravo* achieves a remarkable lyric density.

For example, in one succession of scenes, Hawks combines multiple actions and relationships so subtly that the viewer barely notices their development. While Chance (John Wayne) talks to Stumpy (Walter Brennan) about when he thinks Nathan Burdett will make a move to free his brother, Joe, whom they're holding in the jail (1), Chance mechanically flips through a stack of handbills and wanted circulars. He picks one out and stuffs it in his pocket (2) as he takes Dude (Dean Martin), suffering from the symptoms of alcoholic withdrawal, out on a patrol of the town. Chance's concern for Dude (3), shown in Hawks's slow track-in on the deputy from the sheriff's point-of-view, prompts Chance to use action and professionalism as therapy for his friend. The patrol takes them to the Alamo Hotel where Chance learns that a friend of his, Pat Wheeler (Ward Bond), has put himself in danger by trying to recruit men to help Chance against the Burdetts (1). While he talks to Pat, Chance picks up and examines a deck of cards that had been used in a still-ongoing card game. When Feathers (Angie Dickinson) leaves the game, he pursues her and confronts her with the short deck and the handbill (2). As Chance follows her upstairs, Hawks cuts to a reaction shot of Dude watching them, perhaps remembering the cause of his drunken downfall (3), a woman who, like Feathers, came to town on the stage; who was "no good"; who left him and broke his spirit. Intertwining three stories (the Burdetts, Feathers, Dude) into one continuous action, Hawks weaves all the events and characters into a single fabric. Yet the action does not seem forced; it all happens naturally and logically. Chance acts, at all times, the sheriff he is. It is part of his job to take care of the Burdetts himself, without help; to chase card sharks out of town; and to help Dude, his deputy and friend, rehabilitate himself. Nevertheless, the density of the action takes the film beyond a mere description of what it is like to be sheriff in a small, western town. The film makes a complex statement about the inter-relatedness of every character and every action with every other character and action.

Red River and *The Big Sky* have single-action narratives: the characters in each film are grouped by virtue of their common goals or objectives, the cattle drive and the trading expedition. In both these films, the men are tied together by their participation in the same events. The characters define themselves in terms of their relationships to these events. The number of different actions, stories and relationships in *Rio Bravo* gives it a density that distinguishes it

RIO BRAVO: Colorado (Ricky Nelson) helps Chance (John Wayne) out of a tight spot by tossing him his rifle and joining him in a shoot-out

from Hawks's other westerns from *Red River* through *Rio Lobo*. Yet its images have an iconographic simplicity that undercuts the complexity of the plot and of character interaction. The film's images, set against static backgrounds, usually two intersecting walls, appear simple. At the same time, the characters who stand in front of these static backgrounds, turned in upon themselves by the closed nature of their environment, achieve a complexity that belies the seeming simplicity of the film's images. Shut off from the world around him by the enclosing walls, Dude pounds his leg, translating the unseen, external tension of the world outside into an internal, convulsive muscular contraction that reveals the physical and emotional pain of his reformation. *Red River*, unlike *Rio Bravo*, contains an exciting, dynamic, open background, full of movement and detail. It tends to amplify and extend the physical movement of its characters with echoing movements in the background. Near the end as Matt walks towards his showdown with Dunson, his trail-hands fall away one by one, emphasising his forward movement and giving weight to an action he must perform himself, without help. Three riders, on the distant horizon, mirror this movement in the foreground, gradually melting into the background until only one remains visible. Hawks creates, through choreography of movement, a harmony that reaffirms the oneness of his characters' movements and those in the world around them.

In *Red River*, Hawks unifies his frames through a co-ordination of the movement within them. In *Rio Bravo* he creates tension through the juxtaposition of restricted foreground movement within a static environment. In *Red River*, when Matt and the herd first reach Abilene, their relationship with their background changes. When Matt enters a trading office to sell Dunson's beef, he remarks on the presence of walls and a ceiling, voicing our unspoken feelings about the dramatic shift to interiors. The whole of *Rio Bravo* works like this interior scene in *Red River*: static backgrounds confine the action and concentrate its characters' movements. Unlike *Red River* and *The Big Sky*, *Rio Bravo* is a film *more obviously* about the foreground characters than about the background events which tie them together.

The increasing confinement of the characters in *Rio Bravo* is reversed in the final, explosive, exterior action sequence. Hawks's characters finally move out of the bars, hotel and jail that previously isolated them from the surrounding world when they step into the open spaces of the town's sunlit streets. Near the Burdett warehouse, Chance, Stumpy, Colorado (Ricky Nelson) and Dude fight from behind broken adobe walls, free from confinement under ceilings. In a climactic outburst of action, they dynamite Burdett and his men out of the protective covering of their stronghold.

The final proof of the film's greater concern for character than for action is its closing scene. *Rio Bravo* does not end when Chance, Dude, Colorado and Stumpy, all knit together into a single, interdependent unit by the action, blow up their enemies. It ends with

RIO BRAVO: Stumpy (Walter Brennan), Dude (Dean Martin), and Colorado (Ricky Nelson). They become one through song

the dissolution of tensions in the interiors, climaxing with a reconciliation between Chance and Feathers whose mutual acceptance and acknowledgement of one another can only come when Chance has regained control over external events.

What makes *Rio Bravo* great is this interdependence of character and action. Hawks completes every action and relationship that he begins; but while treating each fully, he also attends to—at the same time and often in the same action—every other action and relationship in the film. Hawks never isolates a single action, like Dude's pouring his drink back into the bottle, or a single relationship, like Chance's amorous conflicts with Feathers, from the others around them. Hawks's film is not about a single issue, single relationship or single character. Rather, it concerns the integration of all its elements into an intricate organic unit.

HATARI!

Hatari! (1962) is, above all else, an extremely delightful picture. Not in the least pretentious or contrived, the film's naturalness, its relaxed visual style and its easy-going pace make watching it an undeniably pleasant experience. Too often, critics who irrationally associate great art with pain and suffering dismiss *Hatari!* on the grounds that it is "only entertainment." More often, critics find fault with Hawks's other films for similar reasons. Even Hawks's admirers, like Robin Wood, draw a blank on *Hatari!* They write long, dissatisfying and dissatisfied essays explaining, in a serious way, the subtlety of the film's relationships and, in Wood's case, invoking comparisons with recognised artists like D. H. Lawrence to make the film seem artistically respectable.

Wood's genuine desire to convince his readers of Hawks's greatness and his obsession with the belief that art must somehow be redemptive come between him and what *Hatari!* really is. Wood writes that *Hatari!* "is a film that makes one wish, as *Rio Bravo* doesn't, that Hawks were, not perhaps a more conscious artist, but more consciously an artist: in *Hatari!* he has been content to be a relaxed entertainer, and the richness of the material leaves one feeling somewhat dissatisfied that more wasn't done with it—a more rigorous following-through and realising of its implications."[*]

Hatari!'s lack of what Wood calls "a pressing inner necessity," its refusal to become *Rio Bravo,* and the lightness with which it treats such serious issues as self-respect are its major virtues. What is great about *Hatari!* is its obviousness. It is both simple and clear in its images, story and characterisation. It is Hawks at his purest: every element in the film functions naturally and organically; nothing is contrived. Much of *Hatari!*'s uniqueness and beauty is due to the absence of a rigid script. Most of the action and much of the dialogue are improvised. Whatever happens, happens "purely." By liberating his characters from the demands of a rigid script, Hawks has, in a way, made them more pure: his characters react naturally and intuitively to situations and events without plot motivation, unencumbered by the mechanical didacticism of a narrative. The lack of specific plot motivation turns particular actions, characters and situations into universal actions, characters and situations; the result is great simplicity and purity of statement.

Hatari! is full of familiar Hawksian situations. Several of its scenes—especially those involving the integration of outsiders into a central group—and the outline of its story resemble scenes and situations present in *Only Angels Have Wings, Red River* and *Rio Bravo.* Borrowed sequences that were tense or highly dramatic in *Angels, Red River,* or *Rio Bravo* appear in *Hatari!* devoid of all tension. Yet the beauty of *Hatari!* comes precisely from the naturalness with which these scenes occur, from their lack of *dramatic* significance. *Hatari!* is not a film like *Rio Bravo,* filled with climaxes and

---

[*] *Howard Hawks, op. cit.,* p. 138.

turning points; nor does it separate events temporally or even in terms of a moral progression. It does not isolate its characters from one another.

The only real form *Hatari!* adheres to is, as Hawks himself points out, that of "a hunting season, from beginning to end." The film begins with an interrupted attempt to capture a rhinoceros; it concludes, significantly, with the completion of this action at the end of the season. Between the interrupted attempt and the later success which bracket the film, Hawks presents variations of this action: men capture animals; women capture men; men capture women. The film ends, as Robin Wood points out, with an ultimate hunting sequence in which three baby elephants "capture" Dallas (Elsa Martinelli).* Hawks also interweaves into his story a sub-sequence of interruptions: Pockets (Red Buttons) repeatedly and comically breaks up the love scenes between Sean (John Wayne) and Dallas. Hawks concludes this pattern of interruptions in the film's final scene when the elephant crashes in on Sean and Dallas's bed.

The structure of *Hatari!* resembles that of a piece of music. Hawks begins with a situation and each subsequent scene works as a variation on that initial situation. What makes *Hatari!* so delightful to watch is the distinctness of each variation on this initial theme. The repetition is not obtrusive; each scene seems fresh. Hawks accomplishes this by continually reversing situations and roles; and, at the same time he keeps the action flowing from each scene to the next. It is impossible to isolate any single action from the events which surround it, since every incident is part of a larger action. Similarly, no shot in the film stands out from those which surround it. There is nothing in *Hatari!* like that first, low-angle, one-shot of Chance in *Rio Bravo*. Partly this is because *Hatari!* is not about specific actions or characters but rather about the physical unity

* *Howard Hawks, ibid.,* p. 135.

of actions, of the group and of the individual characters with the environment. The film, for example, has very few one-shots; most of the compositions contain two or more characters. And since there are almost no close-ups (excepting those of a few animals), the shooting automatically situates the characters within their environment, tied physically to the natural world around them.

Yet the first scene of the film would seem to contradict this. Although Hawks introduces his characters on their truck in medium shot, he cuts in to medium close-up to show Sean, Pockets, Kurt (Hardy Kruger) and the Indian (Bruce Cabot) in isolation, disengaged from one another and from their backgrounds. Even the exact spatial relationship of the truck and the herding car is unclear. We don't know where everyone is in relation to everyone else. Moreover, this whole introduction is shot very statically with no camera movement. But, though Hawks sets up the scene with static group shots and one-shots, he does this only to accentuate the intensity and immediacy of the action and movements which follow. As Sean looks through his binoculars at the herd of wildebeest, the camera pans on his movement to reveal the environment. The pan's movement from medium (Sean) to long shot (the herd) ties Hawks's characters to their environment physically, with actual movement. As the truck and car move out after the rhino, Hawks pans first with the starting movement of the truck and then with that of the car. As the camera pans with the car, the truck enters the frame in the background—the movement of the truck and the car into the same frame clarifies the relationship between the two, joined together in a single action through the camera's pan. Finally, Hawks cuts to a tracking shot from within the cab of the truck. Our involvement in the action and the characters' movement is complete.

The whole scene works so effectively because it is a unity: Hawks pans and cuts from movement to movement, from Sean's first body movement, to the movement of the cars (a physical extension of the characters' movement), and, finally, to the movement of the rhino as it zig-zags in front of the truck. Though he begins the scene statically, Hawks's editing and camera movement tie all the shots together imperceptibly into one fluid movement. The men no longer remain individuals but are caught up in the movement of their trucks and are tied together through the action of the chase.

Most of the hunting sequences work on a basis of movement, shot with a panning and moving camera. There is so much movement (the herding car, the truck, and the animals) that the characters (reflected in the truck and car) seem to whirl around among the animals in a fluid, constantly changing relationship within this completely non-static environment, exemplified best by the shot of Kurt driving around and through a herd of giraffes. All this movement, coupled with the openness of the space which surrounds the characters, gives the film a sense of freedom and liberation that the action sequences in Hawks's other adventure films lack—to this degree, at any rate. The usual alternation between free, open-air, cathartic action sequences and imprisoning, tense, detailed interior sequences is considerably less convulsive in *Hatari!* than in any other Hawks action film. Though the scenes at the compound seem to be shot statically and the backgrounds seem stable, the openness of the film's interiors makes them seem, if anything, a place not of confinement, but of recuperation and rest. The house, like the jail during the song sequence in *Rio Bravo,* is an area of security. The atmosphere of *Hatari!*'s interiors is closer to that of its exteriors and transitions from one to the other are easier than in any other Hawks adventure film. Even the customary inhabitants of Hawksian interiors, women, move simply from the one to the other, taking an active part in the action sequences.

It is precisely because *Hatari!* lacks the tensions and complexities of *Rio Bravo* that it can integrate its characters completely into their environment and relate them with a rare equality to each other without the tensions that interdependence usually creates. *Hatari!* is the summation of all the films that precede it. The same scenes and situations are there that we have seen in other films, but their presence in *Hatari!* is so generalised that each repeated scene or "borrowed" situation is reduced to its pure state. Because Hawks eliminates the sort of dramatic elements that usually distinguish one event from another, every action, character and situation flows into every other action, character and situation. *Hatari!* both simplifies and unifies its elements and, as a result, becomes the purest sort of Hawks film.

EL DORADO and RIO LOBO

If the tight narrative intricacy of *Rio Bravo* preserves the Aristotelian unities of time, place and action, *El Dorado* (1966) and *Rio Lobo* (1970), more loosely structured films, maintain only the unity of action, binding different characters together through their mutual involvement in a series of interrelated events. As a result, *Rio Bravo*'s immediacy and intensity give way to a more relaxed, expansive fluidity and grace that characterise Hawks's recent style and reflect the director's growing oneness with and acceptance of the natural world.

Rio Bravo's sense of slowly elapsing time, felt most vividly in Dude's increasingly greater struggle to regain control of his own body and do his job, contributes to the film's overall intensity, building to a number of progressively dramatic climaxes. In the film's unbroken succession of events and character interactions, each moment is as tense as or more tense than the last, subjecting its characters to a spiralling, nerve-racking pressure. In *El Dorado*

Opposite: EL DORADO: J. P. Harrah (Robert Mitchum) and Cole Thornton (John Wayne) prepare for a gun fight with Jason's men in spite of their own wounds

and *Rio Lobo*, Hawks breaks the major action into two parts separated by a span of time. Reverting to a more paratactic style that separates each action, Hawks frees his characters from the linear momentum of uninterrupted events and enables them to react more easily to each event and function more independently of the action that precedes and follows it. Hawks still relates each individual action to those surrounding it but connects them tangentially rather than directly.

Hawks's most recent films release his characters not only from temporal but also spatial pressures. The strong sense of place in *Rio Bravo*, especially felt in the characters' confinement in interiors, makes its frames seem closed and tight. The film begins at night with a medium close-up of Dude entering a dimly-lit bar through a back door, immediately plunging us into an interior world full of tensions. *El Dorado* and *Rio Lobo* begin outdoors in the bright sunlight—one with shots of J. P. Harrah (Robert Mitchum) walking down the middle of a city street, the other with an elaborate train robbery setpiece, shot in exteriors. Though *El Dorado* progresses towards interiors and the night, *Rio Lobo* plants its characters out of doors and keeps them there, allowing them to retreat to sheltered interiors only at night. Daylit, open frames and the omnipresence of the natural world in these later films give Hawks's characters a greater ease and sureness in their environment. The shots of Col. McNally (John Wayne) riding ahead of his cavalry troop along the railroad tracks or riding upstream in pursuit of stolen union gold convey a sense of his oneness with the natural world that the inhabitants of *Rio Bravo*'s interiors lack. And characters in both later films seem more responsive to the natural landscapes around them. In *El Dorado*, characters appear vulnerable to their natural environment and to natural process, to pain and age. Thornton's failing powers, seen in his slowness and in the bullet wound which paralyses him, contrast sharply with Chance's physical strength and infallibility. While Chance controls his environment by withdrawing from it, Thornton blends with his. He becomes both its victim (during the paralytic attacks) and its ally; in the final shoot-out, Thornton uses his physical disabilities and the cover of night to defeat McLeod.

The victory of the crippled Thornton and Harrah over the healthy McLeod and his men originates in the nature of their alliance. Just as Nathan Burdett's attempts to free his no-good brother Joe inversely mirror Chance's efforts to rehabilitate Dude (the parallel is made visually clear in the final trade of Joe for Dude), so the professional bonds that link McLeod to Bart Jason function as inverted reflections of the deeper, more personal obligations that unite Thornton, Harrah, Mississippi (James Caan) and the Mac-Donalds. *El Dorado* deals more openly than any other Hawks film with the conflict between personal and professional loyalty, externalising it into Thornton's and Jason's opposing factions. Thornton rejects his professional contract with Jason not only because Jason was in the wrong but because he didn't want to fight against Harrah, an old friend. He returns to El Dorado both because he "owes" the MacDonalds and because J.P. needs his help. Mississippi avenges the murder of his friend, Johnny Diamond, and then joins Thornton on a similar mission involving loyalty to a friend. Mississippi also owes Thornton. As he explains his reasons for following Cole, Mississippi adds, "Maybe I could help. You saved my life twice." Thornton quips back, "Yeah, but I'll be too busy to keep doing that." When Joey kills Jason at the end, saving Thornton, she tells Cole that she "owed" him, her bullet having been the initial cause of his paralysis. The involved system of personal loyalties and obligations, present even in the beautifully understated love triangle between Maudie (Charlene Holt), Cole and J.P., creates a strong and complex network of allegiances. It also injects emotional and moral elements into the freely-drawn alliance of Thornton and his friends, compensating for their physical disabilities and proving a crucial factor in their defeat of physically more perfect opponents.

Though Mcleod's professionalism gives him more dignity than any other Hawks villain, the absence of any deeper, more personal obligation on his part condemns him. In the context of the film, each character's survival depends on the help he gets from his friends. In the final analysis, *El Dorado* releases its characters from the traditional conflict of loyalties between their jobs and their personal lives and constructs its more relaxed narrative around the strong friendships that hold characters together. Its openness and the slow, easy movement to its conclusion give its characters time to get to know one another, to work and have fun together. The inner tensions in *Rio Bravo*'s Chance-Dude and Chance-Feathers relationships have no counterpart in *El Dorado*. The harmonious camaraderie of the characters in the latter film marks the emergence of a gracefully articulated, deeply-felt serenity in Hawks's work, yet preserves the humour and vitality that give life to his art.

It is tempting to view Hawks's three most recent John Wayne-Leigh Brackett westerns as a trilogy, organised less around a single thematic concern than around recurrent situations and variations on these situations unified by Wayne's evolutionary relationship to them. The films appear determined more by Wayne's physical strength and age than anything else. As Wayne grows older and his powers fail him, he relies more and more on his friends and employs stratagem rather than strength. At the same time, Wayne's earlier physical power matures into moral strength. In *Rio Bravo*, Chance's physical solidity works as a foil for Dude's weakness. By silently sharing the frame with Dude and reacting to him, Chance gives Dude some of his own strength, enabling him to recover his sobriety and self-respect. Wayne's presence in *Rio Lobo*, though less physically strong, exerts even greater moral weight. At the end of the film, Cord McNally watches as

RIO LOBO: Cord McNally (John Wayne) is presented in the natural world

Amelita (Sherry Lansing) guns down Rio Lobo's corrupt sheriff, "Blue Tom" Hendricks (Mike Henry), and avenges herself for the long, ugly scar Hendricks inflicted on her. McNally, wounded in the leg (for Hawks a sign of physical vulnerability), hobbles over to comfort her. She asks him if what she did was right and he tells her that he would have done it if she hadn't, giving moral sanction to her action. McNally helps Amelita to her feet and they walk off together, leaning on one another for physical and emotional support.

McNally's sensitivity to the emotional needs of others, shown most movingly in his tenderness toward Amelita, reflects Hawks's amplification of the Wayne persona. Hawks makes Wayne the emotional centre of the film, integrating all the characters into one flexible yet cohesive unit through him. Action itself still brings characters together; in the split-second shoot-out in a Blackthorn hotel, Hawks draws Shasta (Jennifer O'Neill), McNally and Cordona (Jorge Rivero) together into a single, well-oiled machine as each automatically comes to the aid of the other. But Wayne's presence in the action gives it an ethical and emotional dimension and makes the characters' union in action moral as well as physical.

Though *Rio Lobo* lacks the density of *Rio Bravo* and the understated grace of *El Dorado,* it has an expansive, loosely articulated undercurrent of shared strength—both physical and moral—that realises itself in the characters' unbidden willingness to help one another. Though it is ultimately Wayne's moral and emotional power that holds the film together, his dependence on the other actors for physical strength, crystallised in the last shot of him and Amelita, sets the seal on his integration into the group. Like Geoff at the end of *Only Angels Have Wings,* McNally needs others as much as they need him.

In one way or another, all of Hawks's films deal with the process of integration. The variety of his work makes this thematic consistency all the more remarkable. No matter what *genre* Hawks operates in—whether he directs mysteries, musicals, westerns, comedies, gangster or science fiction films—his concerns remain the same. Each film, at once characteristic and unique, reveals a new facet of a single vision. The greatness of Hawks's art comes from his ability to give life and richness to each of his films, yet to relate each thematically to the others, augmenting the vitality of his work with a unifying integrity.

HOWARD HAWKS Filmography*

* The information in this filmography is based on material in Jean A. Gili's "Howard Hawks" (Editions Seghers, 1971), Joseph McBride's "Focus on Howard Hawks" (Prentice-Hall, 1972), Robin Wood's "Howard Hawks" (Doubleday/Secker and Warburg, 1968) and "Cahiers du Cinéma," no. 139, Jan. 1963.

Howard Winchester Hawks was born on May 30, 1896 in Goshen, Indiana. Ten years later, the Hawks family moved to California where Howard attended school in Pasadena. He finished secondary school at Philips-Exeter Academy in Massachusetts and, in 1917, graduated from Cornell University with a degree in engineering. During his summer vacations from Cornell, he worked in the property department of the nearby Famous-Players-Lasky Studio (later known as Paramount) and, in 1917, even directed several scenes in Marshall Neilan's *The Little Princess*. After a stint in the Army Air Corps during the First World War, Hawks earned a living by building and flying aeroplanes and by driving race cars. (Years later, in 1936, a Hawks-built car won at Indianapolis.) In 1922, he returned to motion pictures and, as an independent, began to direct and produce two-reel comedies. After working at Paramount and Metro (acquiring original material for scripts and casting a number of pictures), Hawks moved to Fox where he wrote several stories and screenplays, including scripts for Jack Conway's *Quicksands* (1923), George Melford's *Tiger Love* (1924),

Paul Bern's *The Dressmaker from Paris* (1925) and Chester Bennett's *Honesty —The Best Policy* (1926). In the Thirties, Hawks worked on the scripts of several films directed by Victor Fleming, one of his flying buddies, including *Red Dust* (1932), *Captains Courageous* (1937), *Test Pilot* (1938) and *Gone with the Wind* (1939). During the same period, Hawks co-wrote James Cruze's *Sutter's Gold* (1936) and George Stevens's *Gunga Din* (1939); he began shooting on *The Prizefighter and the Lady* (1933) but was replaced early in production by W. S. Van Dyke who got credit for the film. Both of Hawks's brothers worked in the motion picture industry. Kenneth Hawks also worked at Fox in the Twenties as a producer, writer and director (*Big Time, Masked Emotions* in 1929; *Such Men Are Dangerous* in 1930) until his death in a plane crash in 1930. William Hawks produced, among other films, Raoul Walsh's *The Tall Men* (1955), a picture with a story loosely based on that of *Red River*.

Silent Films

THE ROAD TO GLORY (1926). After losing her sight and faith in God in a car accident that took her father's life, a girl leaves her fiancé and retreats to the mountains where her sight and faith are restored after another accident which injures her fiancé. *Sc:* L. G. Rigby (story by Howard Hawks). *Ph:* Joseph August. *With:* May McAvoy (*Judith Allen*), Leslie Fenton (*David Hale*), Ford Sterling

61

(*James Allen*), Rockliffe Fellowes (*Del Cole*), Milla Davenport (*Aunt Selma*), John MacSweeney (*Butler*). *Prod:* William Fox. 6,038 ft. (No prints exist.)

FIG LEAVES (1926). Hawks frames a modern day sex comedy about clothes and fashions with a Keatonesque, Garden of Eden prologue and epilogue in which Eve complains, like her modern counterpart, that she has "nothing to wear." *Sc:* Hope Loring and Louis D. Lighton (story by Howard Hawks). *Ph:* Joseph August (includes two fashion sequences in Technicolor). *Art dir:* William S. Darling and William Cameron Menzies. *Ed:* Rose Smith. *Cost:* Adrian. *With:* George O'Brien (*Adam Smith*), Olive Bordon (*Eve Smith*), Phyllis Haver (*Alice Atkins*), André de Béranger (*Josef André*), William Austin (*André's assistant*), Heinie Conklin (*Eddie McSwiggen*). *Prod:* Howard Hawks for Fox. 6,498 ft.

THE CRADLE SNATCHERS (1927). Comedy. Three wives try to cure their husbands of consorting with flappers by arranging for three college boys to flirt with them at a party. *Sc:* Sarah Mason (based on a play by Russell G. Medcraft and Norma Mitchell). *Ph:* L. William O'Connell. *With:* Louise Fazenda (*Susan Martin,*) J. Farrell MacDonald (*George Martin*), Ethel Wales (*Ethel Drake*), Franklin Pangborn (*Howard Drake*), Dorothy Phillips (*Kitty Ladd*), William Davidson (*Roy Ladd*), Joseph Striker (*Joe Valley*), Nick Stuart (*Henry Winton*), Arthur Lake (*Oscar*). *Prod:* William Fox. 6,281 ft. (No complete prints exist.)

PAID TO LOVE (1927). Comedy. Before an American banker will draft a loan to a bankrupt Balkan kingdom, its misogynistic crown prince must take an interest in women; the banker and the king lure the prince away from his fascination with cars by means of Gaby, a Parisian con artist. *Sc:* William M. Conselman, Seton I. Miller and Benjamin Glazer (story by Harry Carr). *Ph:* L. William O'Connell. *Art dir:* William S. Darling. *Ed:* Ralph Dixon. *With:* George O'Brien (*Crown Prince Michael*), Virginia Valli (*Gaby*), J. Farrell MacDonald (*Peter Roberts*), Thomas Jefferson (*King*), William Powell (*Prince Eric*). *Prod:* Howard Hawks for Fox. 6,888 ft.

A GIRL IN EVERY PORT (1928). Adventure. Two sailors, rivals for girls in ports around the world, meet and become friends. *Sc:* Seton I. Miller, Reginald Morris and James K. McGuinness (story by Howard Hawks). *Ph:* L. William O'Connell and R. J. Berquist. *Art dir:* William S. Darling. *Ed:* Ralph Dixon. *With:* Victor McLaglen (*Spike*), Robert Armstrong (*Bill*), Louise Brooks (*Marie*), Maria Casajuana, Natalie Joyce, Dorothy Mathews, Greta Yoltz, Sally Rand. *Prod:* Howard Hawks for Fox. 5,500 ft.

FAZIL (1928). Melodrama. Two cultures collide when a despotic Arab prince marries a liberated Parisian socialite and forces her to adopt Eastern customs. *Sc:* Seton I. Miller and Philip Klein (based on the play "L'insoumise" by Pierre Frondaie and the English adaptation, "Prince Fazil"). *Ph:* L. William O'Connell. *Ed:* Ralph Dixon. Released with musical score and sound effects. *With:* Charles Farrell (*Prince Fazil*), Greta Nissen (*Fabienne*), Mae Busch (*Hélène Debreuze*), John Boles

(*John Clavering*), Tyler Brooke (*Jacques Debreuze*), Vadim Uraneff (*Ahmed*), Eddie Sturgis (*Rice*), Josephine Borio (*Aicha*). *Prod:* William Fox. 7,217 ft.

THE AIR CIRCUS (1928). A young pilot overcomes his fear of flying in order to rescue his friend and a pretty aviatrix. *Co-dir:* Lewis Seiler. *Sc:* Norman Z. McLeod, Seton I. Miller and Hugh Herbert (story by Graham Baker and Andrew Bennison). *Ph:* Dan Clark. *Ed:* Ralph Dixon. Released with talking sequences, sound effects and a musical score. *With:* Louise Dresser (*Mrs. Blake*), David Rollins (*Buddy Blake*), Arthur Lake (*Speed Doolittle*), Sue Carol (*Sue Manning*), Charles Delaney (*Charles Manning*), Heinie Conklin (*Jerry McSwiggen*), Earl Robinson (*Lt. Blake*). *Prod:* William Fox. 7,702 ft. Seiler was

brought in to direct dialogue sequences that were added to Hawks's silent footage.

TRENT'S LAST CASE (1929). Murder mystery. *Sc:* Scott Darling and Beulah Marie Dix (based on E. C. Bentley's novel). *Ph:* Harold Rosson. Released with sound effects and a musical score. *With:* Donald Crisp (*Sigsbee Manderson*), Raymond Griffith (*Philip Trent*), Raymond Hatton (*Joshua Cupples*), Marceline Day (*Evelyn Manderson*), Lawrence Gray (*Jack Marlowe*), Nicholas Soussanin (*Martin*), Anita Garvin (*Ottilie Dunois*), Ed Kennedy (*Inspector Murch*). *Prod:* William Fox. 5,834 ft. Because it was silent the film was never released in the United States and was shown only in England.

Sound Films

THE DAWN PATROL (1930). An action film telling the story of a squadron of British pilots at the front in the First World War. *Sc:* Howard Hawks, Dan Totheroh and Seton I. Miller (story by John Monk Saunders). *Ph:* Ernest Haller. *Art dir:* Jack Okey. *Ed:* Ray Curtiss. *Mus:* Leo F. Forbstein. *With:* Richard Barthelmess (*Dick Courtney*), Douglas Fairbanks, Jr. (*Douglas Scott*), Neil Hamilton (*Major Brand*), William Janney (*Gordon Scott*), James Finlayson (*Field Sergeant*), Clyde Cook (*Bott*), Gardner James (*Ralph Hollister*), Edmond Breon (*Phipps*), Frank McHugh (*Flaherty*). *Prod:* Robert North for First National-Warner Bros. 95m. The story, credited to Saunders but actually written

by Hawks, won an Academy Award as the best screen story of 1930. The film's title was changed to FLIGHT COMMANDER when Edmund Goulding's remake (which includes action footage from Hawks's film and closely follows his screenplay) was released in 1938.

THE CRIMINAL CODE (1931). Prison drama. A tough district attorney faces the men he sent to prison when he is appointed warden and comes to understand the moral code by which they live. *Sc:* Seton I. Miller, Fred Niblo, Jr. (based on a story by Martin Flavin). *Ph:* James Wong Howe and L. William O'Connell. *Art dir:* Edward Jewell. *Ed:* Edward Curtis. *With:* Walter Huston (*Warden Brady*), Constance Cummings

(*Mary Brady*), Philips Holmes (*Robert Graham*), Mary Doran (*Gertrude Williams*), Boris Karloff (*Galloway*), De Witt Jennings (*Gleason*), John Sheehan (*McManus*), Otto Roffman (*Fales*), Clark Marshall (*Runch*), Arthur Hoyt (*Nettleford*). *Prod:* Howard Hawks and Harry Cohn for Columbia. 97m.

SCARFACE (1932). Subtitled SHAME OF THE NATION. A gangster's rise to the top of the Chicago underworld. *Sc:* Ben Hecht, Seton I. Miller, John Lee Mahin, W. R. Burnett (based on a novel by Armitage Trail). *Ph:* Lee Garmes and L. William O'Connell. *Art dir:* Harry Oliver. *Ed:* Edward Curtis. *Mus:* Adolph Tandler and Gus Arnheim. *With:* Paul Muni (*Tony Camonte*), Ann Dvorak (*Cesca*), Karen Morley (*Poppy*), George Raft (*Guino Rinaldo*), Osgood Perkins (*Johnny Lovo*), Boris Karloff (*Gaffney*), Vince Barnett (*Angelo*), C. Henry Gordon (*Guarino*), Ines Palange (*Mrs. Camonte*), Edwin Maxwell (*Chief of Detectives*), Tully Marshall (*managing editor*), Henry Armetta (*Pietro*), Purnell Pratt (*Publisher*). *Prod:* Howard Hawks and Howard Hughes for Atlantic Pictures. Released by United Artists. 90m. Censorship problems held up the film's release for almost two years (1930–32). Hawks shot two different endings and, after he left the film, the scene in the publisher's office was shot and inserted to appease the censors.

THE CROWD ROARS (1932). A champion race car driver quarrels with his younger brother, also a driver, and inadvertently kills another driver who tries to separate them on the track. *Sc:* Kubec Glasmon, John Bright, Seton I. Miller, Niven Busch (story by Howard

THE CROWD ROARS: Joe Green (James Cagney), Lee (Ann Dvorak), and Anne (Joan Blondell) argue about Joe's kid brother

Hawks). *Ph:* Sid Hickox. *Art dir:* Jack Okey. *Ed:* John Stumar and Thomas Pratt. *Mus:* Leo F. Forbstein. *With:* James Cagney (*Joe Green*), Joan Blondell (*Anne*), Ann Dvorak (*Lee*), Eric Linden (*Eddie Green*), Guy Kibbee (*Dad Greer*), Frank McHugh (*Spud*), William Arnold (*Bill*), Leo Nomis (*Jim*), Charlotte Merriam (*Mrs. Spud Smith*), Harry Hartz, Ralph Hepburn, Fred Guisso, Phil Pardee, Spider Matlock, Jack Brisko, Fred Frame (*Race Drivers*). *Prod:* Warner Bros. 85m. Lloyd Bacon's re-make, *Indianapolis Speedway* (1939), borrows racing footage from Hawks's film.

TIGER SHARK (1932). A Portuguese tuna fisherman marries a girl with whom his best friend later falls in love. *Sc:* Wells Root (from the novel "Tuna" by Houston Branch). *Ph:* Tony Gaudio. *Art dir:* Jack Okey. *Ed:* Thomas Pratt. *Mus:* Leo F. Forbstein. *With:* Edward G. Robinson (*Mike Mascerena*), Richard Arlen (*Pipes Boley*), Zita Johann (*Quita*), Vince Barnett (*Fishbone*), J. Carrol Naish (*Tony*), William Ricciardi (*Manuel Silva*), Leila Bennet (*Lady Barber*). *Prod:* First National-Warner Bros. 80m.

TODAY WE LIVE (1933). War melodrama. A love triangle, complicated by strong bonds of friendship, leads to multiple sacrifices in World War I. *Sc:* William Faulkner, Edith Fitzgerald and Dwight Taylor (from story, "Turnabout," by William Faulkner). *Ph:* Oliver T. Marsh. *Ed:* Edward Curtis. *With:* Joan Crawford (*Diana*), Gary Cooper (*Bogard*), Robert Young (*Claude*), Franchot Tone (*Ronnie*), Roscoe Karns (*McGinnis*), Louise Closser Hale (*Applegate*), Rollo Lloyd (*Major*), Hilda Vaughn (*Eleanor*). *Prod:* Howard Hawks for M-G-M. 113m.

VIVA VILLA! (1934). Story of the popular Mexican bandit and patriot, Pancho Villa. *Dir:* Jack Conway. *Sc:* Ben Hecht and Howard Hawks (story by Edgcumb Pinchon and O. B. Stade). *Ph:* James Wong Howe and Charles G. Clarke. *Art dir:* Harry Oliver. *Ed:* Robert J. Kern. *Mus:* Herbert Stothart. *With:* Wallace Beery (*Pancho Villa*), Leo Carrillo (*Sierra*), Fay Wray (*Teresa*), Donald Cook (*Don Felipe*), Henry B. Walthall (*Madero*), Stuart Erwin (*Johnny Sykes*), George E. Stone (*Emilio Chavito*), Joseph Schildkraut (*General Pascal*), Katherine de Mille (*Rosita*). *Prod:* David O. Selznick for M-G-M. 115m.

Louis Mayer removed Hawks from the picture when he refused to give the studio information regarding an incident with Lee Tracy, one of his actors. Erwin replaced Tracy and Conway Hawks. Hawks directed more than half the film, shooting all the exteriors in Mexico.

TWENTIETH CENTURY (1934). Comedy: A theatrical producer loses his star discovery to the movies but wins her back somewhere between Chicago and New York on the Twentieth Century Limited. *Sc:* Ben Hecht and Charles MacArthur (from a Hecht and MacArthur play based on Charles Bruce Milholland's play, "Napoleon on Broadway"). *Ph:* Joseph Walker and Joseph August. *Ed:* Gene Havlick. *With:* John

TIGER SHARK: Mike (Edward G. Robinson) uses his hook on a man (J. Carrol Naish) who is bothering Quita (Zita Johann)

Barrymore (*Oscar Jaffe*), Carole Lombard (*Lily Garland*), Walter Connolly (*Oliver Webb*), Roscoe Karms (*O'Malley*), Etienne Giradot (*Matthew Clark*), Charles Levison (*Max Jacobs*), Dale Fuller (*Sadie*), Ralph Forbes (*George Smith*), Edgar Kennedy (*McGonigle*). *Prod:* Howard Hawks for Columbia. 91m.

BARBARY COAST (1935). In Nineteenth century San Francisco a girl, partners with an underworld big-shot, meets and falls in love with a poetic prospector. *Sc:* Ben Hecht and Charles MacArthur. *Ph:* Ray June. *Art dir:* Richard Day. *Ed:* Edward Curtis. *Mus:* Alfred Newman. *With:* Miriam Hopkins (*Swan*), Edward G. Robinson (*Louis Chamalis*), Joel McCrae (*James Carmichael*), Walter Brennan (*Old Atrocity*), Frank Craven (*Col. Cobb*), Brian Donlevy (*Knuckles*), Harry Carey (*Slocum*), Clyde Cook (*Oakie*), Donald Meek (*McTavish*). *Prod:* Samuel Goldwyn for Goldwyn Productions. Released by United Artists. 97m.

CEILING ZERO (1935). Mail pilots fight fog, ice and failing powers to stay in the air; a recently grounded, former war ace, indirectly responsible for another pilot's death, takes off on a suicidal flight to test a new de-icer. *Sc:* Frank "Spig" Wead (based on his play). *Ph:* Arthur Edeson. *Art dir:* Richard Day. *Ed:* William Holmes. *Mus:* Leo F. Forbstein. *With:* James Cagney (*Dizzy Davis*), Pat O'Brien (*Jack Lee*), June Travis (*Tommy*), Stuart Erwin (*Texas*), Isabel Jewell (*Lori*), Henry Wadsworth (*Tay*), Craig Reynolds (*Joe Allen*). *Prod:* Harry Joe Brown and Howard Hawks for Cosmopolitan Pictures. Released by Warner Bros. 95m.

THE ROAD TO GLORY (1936). War adventure. A tough French army officer in the First World War breaks in another who falls in love with his girl and is torn between loyalty and love. *Sc:* Joel Sayre and William Faulkner (based on Raymond Bernard's film *Les croix de bois* taken from a novel by Roland Dorgelès). *Ph:* Gregg Toland. *Art dir:* Hans Peters. *Ed:* Edward Curtis. *Mus:* Louis Silvers. *With:* Fredric March (*Lt. Michel Denet*), Warner Baxter (*Capt. Paul Laroche*), Lionel Barrymore (*Papa Laroche*), June Lang (*Monique*), Gregory Ratoff (*Bouffiou*), Victor Kilian (*Régnier*), Paul Stanton (*Relief Captain*), John Qualen (*Duflous*), Paul Fix (*Rigaud*). *Prod:* Darryl F. Zanuck for 20th Century-Fox. 95m.

COME AND GET IT (1936). Story of a Wisconsin lumber magnate who becomes a rival with his son for the love of the daughter of a woman he knew years ago. *Co-dir:* William Wyler. *Sc:* Jules Furthman and Jane Murfin (from a novel by Edna Ferber). *Ph:* Gregg Toland and Rudolph Maté. *Ed:* Edward Curtis. *Mus:* Alfred Newman. *With:* Edward Arnold (*Barney Glasgow*), Joel McCrea (*Richard Glasgow*), Frances Farmer (*Lotta*), Walter Brennan (*Swan Bostrom*), Andrea Leeds (*Evvie Glasgow*), Frank Shields (*Tony Schwerke*), Mady Christians (*Karie*), Mary Nash (*Emma Louise Glasgow*). *Prod:* Samuel Goldwyn for Goldwyn Productions. Released by United Artists. 105m. Hawks directed all but the final ten minutes of the film. Walter Brennan received an Academy Award for Best Supporting Actor.

BRINGING UP BABY (1938). Comedy. An absent-minded paleontologist meets a hair-brained socialite with a pet leopard and becomes "a nut from Brazil" when a dog steals a valuable fossil. *Sc:* Dudley Nichols and Hager Wilde (story by Wilde). *Ph:* Russell Metty. *Art dir:* Van Nest Polglase and Perry Ferguson. *Ed:* George Hively. *Mus:* Roy Webb. *With:* Cary Grant (*David Huxley*), Katharine Hepburn (*Susan*), Charles Ruggles (*Horace Applegate*), Walter Catlett (*Slocum*), Barry Fitzgerald (*Gogarty*), May Robson (*Aunt Elizabeth*), Fritz Feld (*Dr. Lehmann*), Virginia Walker (*Alice Swallow*), George Irving (*Peabody*), Asta (*George, the dog*), Nissa (*Baby, the leopard*). *Prod:* Howard Hawks for RKO. 102m.

ONLY ANGELS HAVE WINGS (1939). Adventure. A group of South American mail pilots fight fog and the Andes to win a government mail contract. *Sc:* Jules Furthman (story by Howard Hawks). *Ph:* Joseph Walker and Elmer Dyer (aerial sequences). *Art dir:* Lionel Banks. *Ed:* Viola Lawrence. *Mus:* Dimitri Tiomkin. *With:* Cary Grant (*Geoff Carter*), Jean Arthur (*Bonnie Lee*), Richard Barthelmess (*Bat McPherson*), Rita Hayworth (*Judith*), Thomas Mitchell (*Kid Dabb*), Sig Rugman (*Dutchie*), Allyn Joslyn (*Les Peters*), Victor Kilian (*Sparks*), John Carrol (*Gent Shelton*), Noah Beery, Jr. (*Joe Souther*), Donald Barry (*Tex*). *Prod:* Howard Hawks for Columbia. 121m.

HIS GIRL FRIDAY (1940). Comedy. A delightfully unscrupulous editor wins back his star reporter and wife by involving her in a fast-breaking news story. *Sc:* Charles Lederer (from Ben Hecht's and Charles MacArthur's play,

"The Front Page." *Ph:* Joseph Walker. *Art dir:* Lionel Banks. *Ed:* Gene Havlick. *Mus:* Morris Stoloff. *With:* Cary Grant (*Walter Burns*), Rosalind Russell (*Hildy Johnson*), Ralph Bellamy (*Bruce Baldwin*), Gene Lockhart (*Sheriff Hartwell*), Porter Hall (*Murphy*), Ernest Truex (*Bensiger*), Clarence Kolb (*Mayor*), Roscoe Karns (*McCue*), Frank Jenks (*Wilson*), Regis Toomey (*Sanders*), Abner Biberman (*Diamond Louie*), Frank Orth (*Duffy*), John Qualen (*Earl Williams*), Helen Mack (*Mollie Malloy*), Alma Kruger (*Mrs. Baldwin*). *Prod:* Howard Hawks for Columbia. 92m.

THE OUTLAW (1940). Western. Story of Doc Holliday, Billy the Kid and Pat Garrett. *Dir:* Howard Hughes. *Sc:* Jules Furthman. *Ph:* Gregg Toland. *Ed:* Wallace Grissell. *Mus:* Victor Young. *With:* Jane Russell (*Rio McDonald*), Walter Huston (*Doc Holliday*), Jack Buetel (*Billy the Kid*), Thomas Mitchell (*Pat Garrett*), Joe Sawyer (*Charlie*). *Prod:* Howard Hughes for Hughes Productions. Released by RKO. 123m. Hawks worked for ten days directing the picture.

SERGEANT YORK (1941). War adventure. A biographical account of the First World War's most famous American hero. *Sc:* Abem Finkel, Harry Chandler, Howard Koch, John Huston (from the Diary of Sergeant York as edited by Tom Skeyhill). *Ph:* Sol Polito and Arthur Edeson (battle sequences). *Art dir:* John Hughes. *Ed:* William Holmes. *Mus:* Max Steiner. *With:* Gary Cooper (*Alvin C. York*), Walter Brennan (*Pastor Rosier Pile*), Joan Leslie (*Gracie Williams*), George Tobias ("*Pusher*" *Rose*), Stanley Ridges (*Major Buxton*), Margaret Wy-

SERGEANT YORK: Gary Cooper leads his prisoners-of-war back to his own lines

cherley (*Mother York*), Ward Bond (*Ike Botkin*), Noah Beery, Jr. (*Buck Lipscomb*), June Lockhart (*Rosie York*), Dickie Moore (*George York*), Clem Bevans (*Zeke*), Howard de Silva (*Lem*), Charles Trowbridge (*Cordell Hull*). *Prod:* Jesse L. Lasky and Hal B. Wallis for Warner Bros. 134m. Gary Cooper won the Academy Award for Best Actor.

BALL OF FIRE (1941). Comedy. Professors working on a slang entry for an encyclopaedia unwittingly provide a hide-out for a singer wanted by the police for questioning. *Sc:* Billy Wilder and Charles Brackett (from story, "From A to Z," by Wilder and Thomas Monroe). *Ph:* Gregg Toland. *Art dir:* Perry Ferguson. *Ed:* Daniel Mandell. *Mus:* Alfred Newman. *With:* Gary Cooper (*Bertram Potts*), Barbara Stanwyck (*Sugarpuss O'Shea*), Oscar Homolka (*Prof. Gurkakoff*), Dana Andrews (*Joe Lilac*), Dan Duryea (*Duke Pastrami*), Henry Travers (*Prof. Jerome*), S. Z. Sakall (*Prof. Magenbruch*), Tully Marshall (*Prof. Robinson*), Leonid Kinskey (*Prof. Quintana*), Richard Haydn (*Prof. Oddly*), Aubrey Mather (*Prof. Peagram*), Allen Jenkins (*Garbage Man*) and Gene Krupa and his Band. *Prod:* Samuel Goldwyn for Goldwyn Productions. Released by RKO. 111m.

AIR FORCE (1943). The story of an Army Air Force B-17 bomber and its crew during the first few weeks of the Second World War in the Pacific. *Sc:* Dudley Nichols and William Faulkner.

AIR FORCE: Gig Young, Sgt. White (Harry Carey) and Capt. Quincannon (John Ridgely)

Ph: James Wong Howe and Elmer Dyer, Charles Marshall (aerial sequences). *Art dir:* John Hughes. *Ed:* George Amy. *Mus:* Franz Waxman. *With:* John Garfield (*Winocki*), John Ridgely (*Capt. Quincannon*), George Tobias (*Cpl. Weinberg*), Harry Carey (*Sgt. White*), Gig Young (*Lt. Williams*), Arthur Kennedy (*Lt. McMartin*), James Brown (*Lt. Rader*), Charles Drake, Ward Wood, Ray Montgomery. *Prod:* Hal B. Wallis and Howard Hawks for Warner Bros. 124m. George Amy won an Academy Award for Best Film Editing.

CORVETTE K-225 (1943). Canadian navy in Second World War. *Dir:* Richard Rosson. *Sc:* Lt. John Rhodes Sturdy. *Ph:* Tony Gaudio and Harry Perry. *Art dir:* John B. Goodman and Robert Boyle. *Ed:* Edward Curtis. *Mus:* David Buttolph. *With:* Randolph Scott, Ella Raines, Barry Fitzgerald, James Brown, Andy Devine, Noah Beery, Jr., Fuzzy Knight, Richard Lane, Thomas Gomez, Robert Mitchum. *Prod:* Howard Hawks for Universal. 99m. Hawks cast the picture, worked on the script and supervised the shooting.

TO HAVE AND HAVE NOT (1944). Charterboat captain in Martinique, left broke when his client is accidentally killed in a Gestapo raid, becomes involved with an itinerant showgirl and the Free French forces on the island. *Sc:* Jules Furthman and William Faulkner (loosely based on a novel by Ernest Hemingway). *Ph:* Sid Hickox. *Art dir:* Charles Novi. *Ed:* Christian Nyby. *Mus:* Leo F. Forbstein (songs by Hoagy Carmichael and Johnny Mercer). *With:* Humphrey Bogart (*Harry Morgan*), Walter Brennan (*Eddie*), Lauren Bacall

TO HAVE AND HAVE NOT: the Gestapo chief (Dan Seymour) tells Harry Morgan (Humphrey Bogart) that he is holding Eddie prisoner. Slim (Lauren Bacall) and Frenchy (Marcel Dalio) look on

(*Slim*), Dolores Moran (*Hélène de Bursac*), Hoagy Carmichael (*Crickett*), Walter Molnar (*Paul de Bursac*), Sheldon Leonard (*Lt. Coyo*), Marcel Dalio (*Frenchy Gérard*), Walter Sande (*Johnson*), Dan Seymour (*Capt. Reynard*). *Prod:* Howard Hawks for Warner Bros. 100m.

THE BIG SLEEP (1946). A hard-boiled detective's blackmail investigation results in a complicated series of murders and in a love affair with his client's daughter. *Sc:* William Faulkner, Leigh Brackett and Jules Furthman (from a novel by Raymond Chandler). *Ph:* Sid Hickox. *Art dir:* Carl Jules Weyl. *Ed:* Christian Nyby. *Mus:* Max Steiner. *With:* Humphrey Bogart (*Philip Marlowe*),

Lauren Bacall (*Vivian*), John Ridgely (*Eddie Mars*), Martha Vickers (*Carmen*), Dorothy Malone (*Bookshop Girl*), Regis Toomey (*Bernie Ohls*), Bob Steele (*Canino*), Elisha Cook, Jr. (*Jones*), Charles Waldren (*Gen. Sternwood*), Charles D. Brown (*Norris*), Louis Jean Heydt (*Joe Brody*), Sonia Darrin (*Agnes*). *Prod:* Howard Hawks for Warner Bros. 114m.

RED RIVER (1948). An epic western telling of the men who made the first cattle drive up the Chisholm Trail from Texas to Kansas. *Sc:* Borden Chase and Charles Schnee (from novel by Chase). *Ph:* Russell Harlan. *Art dir:* John Datu Arensma. *Ed:* Christian Nyby. *Mus:* Dimitri Tiomkin. *With:* John Wayne (*Tom Dunson*), Montgomery Clift (*Matthew Garth*), Joanne Dru (*Tess Millay*), Walter Brennan (*Groot*), Coleen Gray (*Fen*), John Ireland (*Cherry*), Noah Beery, Jr. (*Buster*), Chief Yowlachie (*Quo*), Harry Carey, Sr. (*Melville*), Harry Carey, Jr. (*Dan Latimer*), Hank Worden (*Sims*), Paul Fix (*Teeler*). *Prod:* Howard Hawks for Monterey Productions. Released by United Artists. 125m.

A SONG IS BORN (1948). Musical comedy. Scholars working on an encyclopaedia of music provide a hide-out for a gangster's moll. *Sc:* Harry Tugent (basd on Hawks's "Ball of Fire"). *Ph:* Gregg Toland (Technicolor). *Art dir:* George Jenkins and Perry Ferguson. *Ed:* Daniel Mandell. *Mus:* Emil Newman and Hugo Friedhofer (songs by Don Raye and Gene De Paul). *With:* Danny Kaye (*Prof. Frisbee*), Virginia Mayo (*Honey Swanson*), Benny Goodman (*Prof. Magenbruch*), Hugh Herbert (*Prof. Twingle*), Steve Cochran (*Tony Crow*), J.

Edward Bromberg (*Dr. Elfini*), Felix Bressart (*Prof. Gurkakoff*), Ludwig Stossel (*Prof. Traumer*), O. Z. Whitehead (*Prof. Oddly*), Esther Dale (*Miss Bragg*), Mary Field (*Miss Totten*) and Tommy Dorsey, Louis Armstrong, Lionel Hampton, Charlie Barnett, Mel Powell, Buck and Bubbles. *Prod:* Samuel Goldwyn for Goldwyn Productions. Released by RKO. A re-make of *Ball of Fire* (1941).

I WAS A MALE WAR BRIDE (YOU CAN'T SLEEP HERE) (1949). Comedy. After the Second World War, a French officer becomes entangled in U.S. Army red tape when he tries to marry an American lieutenant. *Sc:* Charles Lederer, Leonard Spigelgass and Hagar Wilde (from a novel by Henri Rochard). *Ph:* Norbert Brodine and O. H. Borradaile. *Art dir:* Lyle Wheeler and Albert Hogsett. *Ed:* James B. Clark. *Mus:* Cyril Mockridge. *With:* Cary Grant (*Henri Rochard*), Ann Sheridan (*Catherine Gates*), William Neff (*Capt. Jack Rumsey*), Engene Gericke (*Tony Jowitt*), Marion Marshall (*Kitty*), Kenneth Tobey (*Red*). *Prod:* Sol. C. Siegel for 20th Century-Fox. 105m.

THE THING (FROM ANOTHER WORLD) (1951). Science fiction. Scientists at the North Pole discover a creature from another world. *Dir:* Christian Nyby. *Sc:* Charles Lederer and Howard Hawks (story by John Wood Campbell Jr.). *Ph:* Russell Harlan. *Art dir:* Albert S. D'Agostino. *Ed:* Roland Cross. *Mus:* Dimitri Tiomkin. *With:* Margaret Sheridan (*Nikki*), Kenneth Tobey (*Capt. Hendry*), Robert Cornthwaite (*Prof. Carrington*), Douglas Spencer (*Skeely*), James Young (*Lt.*

Dykes), Dewey Martin (*Crew Chief*), Robert Nichols (*Lt. Erickson*), James Arness (*The Thing*). *Prod:* Howard Hawks for Winchester Productions. Released by RKO. 87m. Hawks worked on the script, with the actors and closely supervised the shooting.

THE BIG SKY (1952). Western. An expedition poles a keelboat up the Missouri River to trade with the Blackfeet Indians. *Sc:* Dudley Nichols (from a novel by A. B. Guthrie, Jr.). *Ph:* Russell Harlan. *Art dir:* Albert S. D'Agostino and Perry Ferguson. *Ed:* Christian Nyby. *Mus:* Dimitri Tiomkin. *With:* Kirk Douglas (*Jim Deakins*), Dewey Martin (*Boone Caudill*), Elizabeth Threatt (*Teal Eye*), Arthur Hunnicutt (*Zeb Calloway*), Steven Geray (*Jourdonnais*), Hank Worden (*Poordevil*), Buddy Baer (*Romaine*), Jim Davis (*Streak*), Henri Letondal (*Labadie*), Robert Hunter (*Chouquette*). *Prod:* Howard Hawks for Winchester Productions. Released by RKO. 122m. Shortly after its initial release the film was cut from 140 minutes to 122.

THE RANSOM OF RED CHIEF (from O. HENRY'S FULL HOUSE, 1952). Comedy. Two small-time con men kidnap a boy who turns the tables on them, holds them prisoner and forces them to pay him ransom money. *Sc:* Nunnally Johnson (from a story by O. Henry). *Ph:* Milton Krasner. *Art dir:* Chester Goce. *Mus:* Alfred Newman. *With:* Fred Allen (*Sam*), Oscar Levant (*Bill*), Lee Aaker (*J.B.*), Kathleen Freeman (*J.B.'s Mother*), Alfred Minor (*J.B.'s Father*). *Prod:* André Hakim for 20th Century-Fox. 20m. Hawks directed the fourth of five sketches in the film.

Kirk Douglas (at right) in THE BIG SKY

MONKEY BUSINESS (1952). Comedy. An industrial scientist experiments with a youth-restoring drug. *Sc:* Ben Hecht, I. A. L. Diamond and Charles Lederer (story by Harry Segall). *Ph:* Milton Krasner. *Art dir:* Lyle Wheeler and George Patrick. *Ed:* William B. Murphy. *Mus:* Leigh Harline. *With:* Cary Grant (*Barnaby Fulton*), Ginger Rogers (*Edwina Fulton*), Charles Coburn (*Mr. Oxly*), Marilyn Monroe (*Lois Laurel*), Hugh Marlowe (*Hank Entwhistle*), Henri Letondal (*Dr. Kitzel*), Robert Cornthwaite (*Dr. Zoldeck*), George Winslow (*Deep-voiced boy*). *Prod:* Sol C. Siegel for 20th Century-Fox. 97m.

GENTLEMEN PREFER BLONDES (1953). Musical comedy. A gold-digging showgirl embarks for Paris with her best friend; a detective, hired by her rich *fiancé's* father, follows her and falls in love with her friend. *Sc:* Charles Lederer (from the musical by Anita Loos and Joseph Fields). *Ph:* Harry J. Wild (Technicolor). *Art dir:* Lyle Wheeler and Joseph C. Wright. *Ed:* Hugh S. Fowler. *Mus:* Jules Styne, Leo Robin, Hoagy Carmichael and Harold Adamson. *With:* Jane Russell (*Dorothy*), Marilyn Monroe (*Lorelei*), Charles Coburn (*Sir Francis Beekman*), Elliott Reid (*Malone*), Tommy Noonan (*Gus Esmond*), George Winslow (*Henry Spofford III*). *Prod:* Sol C. Siegel for 20th Century-Fox. 91m.

LAND OF THE PHARAOHS (1955). Historical epic. A pharaoh commissions a pyramid to be built to celebrate his achievements. *Sc:* William Faulkner, Harry Kurnitz and Harold Jack Bloom. *Ph:* Lee Garmes (interiors) and Russell Harlan (exteriors) (CinemaScope and Warnercolor). *Art dir:* Alexandre Trauner. *Ed:* V. Sagovsky and Rudi Fehr. *Mus:* Dimitri Tiomkin. *With:* Jack Hawkins (*Cheops, the Pharaoh*), Joan Collins (*Princess Nellifer*), Dewey Martin (*Senta*), James Robertson Justice (*Vastar*), Luisa Boni (*Kyra*), Sydney Chaplin (*Treneh*). *Prod:* Howard Hawks for Continental Company. Released by Warner Bros. 106m.

RIO BRAVO (1959). Western. A sheriff holds a murderer prisoner in his jail and waits for the arrival of the U.S. Marshal. *Sc:* Jules Furthman and Leigh Brackett (story by B. H. McCampbell). *Ph:* Russell Harlan (Technicolor, widescreen). *Art dir:* Leo K. Kuter. *Ed:* Folmar Blangsted. *Mus:* Dimitri Tiomkin. *With:* John Wayne (*John T. Chance*), Dean Martin (*Dude*), Ricky Nelson (*Colorado*), Angie Dickinson (*Feathers*), Walter Brennan (*Stumpy*), Ward Bond (*Pat Wheeler*), John Russell (*Nathan Burdett*), Pedro Gonzalez-Gonzalez (*Carlos*), Estelita Rodriguez (*Consuela*), Claude Akins (*Joe Burdett*). *Prod:* Howard Hawks for Armada Productions. Released by Warner Bros. 141m.

HATARI! (1962). Adventure. A group of professional hunters and two women catch wild animals in Africa for European and American zoos. *Sc:* Leigh Brackett (story by Harry Kurnitz). *Ph:* Russell Harlan (Technicolor, widescreen). *Art dir:* Hal Pereira and Carl Anderson. *Ed:* Stuart Gilmore. *Mus:* Henry Mancini. *With:* John Wayne (*Sean Mercer*), Elsa Martinelli (*Dallas*), Hardy Kruger (*Kurt*), Gérard Blain (*Chips*), Red Buttons (*Pockets*), Bruce Cabot (*Indian*), Michèle Girardon (*Brandy*), Valentin de Vargas (*Luis*). *Prod:* Howard Hawks for Malabar Productions. Released by Paramount. 159m.

MAN'S FAVORITE SPORT? (1963). Comedy. An armchair fishing expert (who has never fished before) is blackmailed into entering a fishing contest. *Sc:* John Fenton, Murray and Steve McNeil (story by Pat Frank). *Ph:* Russell Harlan (Technicolor, widescreen). *Art dir:* Alexander Golitzen and Tambi Larsen. *Ed:* Stuart Gilmore. *Mus:* Henry Mancini. *With:* Rock Hudson (*Roger Willoughby*), Paula Prentiss (*Abigail Page*), Maria Perschy (*Easy*), John McGiver (*William Cadwalader*), Charlene Holt (*Tex Conners*), Roscoe Karns (*Major Phipps*), Norman Alden (*John Screaming Eagle*), Forrest Lewis

(*Skaggs*). *Prod:* Howard Hawks for Gibraltar Productions and Laurel Productions. Released by Universal. 127m.

RED LINE 7000 (1965). Racing adventure. A group of stock car drivers and their girls are set off by a series of professional and personal conflicts. *Sc:* Howard Hawks and George Kirgo. *Ph:* Milton Krasner (Technicolor, widescreen). *Art dir:* Hal Pereira and Arthur Lonergan. *Ed:* Stuart Gilmore and Bill Brame. *Mus:* Nelson Riddle (songs by Hoagy Carmichael, Harold Adamson, Nelson Riddle and Carol Conners). *With:* James Caan (*Mike Marsh*), Laura Devon (*Julie Kazarian*), Gail Hire (*Holly MacGregor*), Charlene Holt (*Lindy Bonaparte*), John Robert Crawford (*Ned Arp*), Marianna Hill (*Gaby*), James Ward (*Dan McCall*), Norman Alden (*Pat Kazarian*), George Takei (*Kato*). *Prod:* Howard Hawks for Laurel Productions. Released by Paramount. 127m.

EL DORADO (1967). An aging gunfighter repays several old debts by helping El Dorado's sheriff arrest and hold prisoner a ruthless land baron. *Sc:* Leigh Brackett (based on Harry Brown's novel, "The Stars in Their Courses"). *Ph:* Harold Rosson (Technicolor, widescreen). *Art dir:* Hal Pereira and Carl Anderson. *Ed:* John Woodcock. *Mus:* Nelson Riddle. *With:* John Wayne (*Cole Thornton*), Robert Mitchum (*J. P. Har-*

rah), James Caan (*Mississippi*), Charlene Holt (*Maudie*), Michele Carey (*Joey MacDonald*), Arthur Hunnicutt (*Bull*), R. G. Armstrong (*Kevin MacDonald*), Edward Asner (*Bart Jason*), Paul Fix (*Doc Miller*), Christopher George (*Nelse McLeod*), Johnny Crawford (*Luke MacDonald*). *Prod:* Howard Hawks for Paramount and Laurel Productions. Released by Paramount. 126m. Made in 1966, the film was not released until 1967.

RIO LOBO (1970). Western. A former Union officer assists his Confederate friends in their fight against a Yankee carpetbagger and a corrupt sheriff. *Sc:* Burton Wohl and Leigh Brackett (story by Wohl). *Ph:* William H. Clothier (Technicolor, widescreen). *Art dir:* William R. Kiernan. *Ed:* John Woodcock. *Mus:* Jerry Goldsmith. *With:* John Wayne (*Cord McNally*), Jorge Rivero (*Pierre Cordona*), Jennifer O'Neill (*Shasta*), Jack Elam (*Phillips*), Chris Mitchum (*Tuscarora*), Victor French (*Ketcham*), Susana Dosamantes (*Maria*), Mike Henry (*Sheriff Hendricks*), Bill Williams (*Sheriff Cronin*), Amelita (*Sherry Lansing*), Jim Davis (*Riley*), David Huddleston (*Dr. Jones*), Hank Worden, Edward Faulkner, Peter Jason. *Prod:* Howard Hawks for Malabar Productions. Released by National General Pictures. 114m.

From the title credits of CHINA DOLL

Frank Borzage

*"They are all gone into the world of light!"**

Frank Borzage's critical reputation as a director, built initially on his tremendously successful series of pictures with Charles Farrell and Janet Gaynor at Fox in the Twenties, slowly fell during the Thirties, Forties and Fifties to near anonymity at the time of his death in 1962. *Seventh Heaven* won Borzage an Academy Award as best director at the first awards ceremony in 1927, and he won another for his direction of *Bad Girl* (1931). The undeserved obscurity of Borzage's subsequent work is typified by the fact that critics consider his best sound film to be the Lubitsch-produced *Desire* (1936), a film stylistically and thematically more typical of Lubitsch than Borzage.

With a more representative selection of the director's work now available, it is possible to see how great and how totally misunderstood Borzage was. Looking at *Desire* in the context of his other films provides a good illustration of what Borzage is not and helps to clarify the nature of Borzage's concerns. Throughout the film, Lubitsch's wit and cynicism work at cross purposes against Borzage's lyrical romanticism. Lubitsch's sophisticated wit irreverently jokes with traditional notions of morality and, at the same time, denies the essential humanity of his characters, identifying them with objects or with artificial surfaces and textures in their environment. At the beginning of *Desire*, Madeleine (Marlene Dietrich) appears, dressed in white, riding in a pure white limousine. In the next scene, her black clothes exactly match the shade of her black limousine. Like the black-on-white character *décor* idea in the widow Sonia's room in *The Merry Widow* (1934), Lubitsch's outrageous extremes put his characters on a level with their *décor*,

---

* The first line of Henry Vaughan's "Ascension Hymn."

explaining them through their surrounding architecture and integrating them into its tremendously stylised surface.

Later in *Desire,* Lubitsch, re-working the earlier limousine gag, uses two cars to symbolise the start of a sexual-romantic relationship between his central characters. Tom (Gary Cooper) accidentally bumps his Bronson-8 into Madeleine's limousine in traffic. Later, on the road to Spain, Madeleine's sports car speeds past Tom, covering him with dust. Lubitsch's architectural view of characters translates their actions mechanistically: the movement and choreography of the cars on the highway suggest the characters' sexual antagonism and attraction.

Borzage's direction of this bit of Lubitsch business has the effect of personalising the action: his romantic close-ups work against the depersonalised action in long shot. Where Lubitsch's winking visual puns and conceits reveal a view of the world that is deeply cynical in outlook, Borzage's innocent, unblinking eye and visual simplicity make him seem naïve by contrast. The straightforward purity of Borzage's outlook demands that his characters and their situation be taken seriously and permits him a broader range of emotional expression than cynically incredulous directors like Lubitsch allow themselves. While Lubitsch laughs at melodramatic technique and convention, Borzage sees a truth in its vision: as a narrative director, he believes in melodrama as a way of seeing the world.

One of the reasons that melodrama—and great film-makers like D. W. Griffith and Borzage who work within its conventions—remains in critical disrepute is that, as a form, it tends to externalise, to transform a character's inner conflicts into external events.° Nineteenth-century melodramatic literature traditionally presents

---

° Corrigan, Robert W., ed., "Laurel British Drama: The Nineteenth Century," New York, Dell Publishing Co., 1967, pp. 7–8.

Opposite: Frank Borzage as actor in a silent film. Title unknown

two-dimensional characters caught up in a melodramatic situation, often at the mercy of a hostile environment or of an extension of that environment, such as a villain. Though the *genre's* lack of complexity has a primitive sort of purity to it, this simplicity becomes, if handled poorly, its chief drawback. The best melodramatic literature—that of Dickens, Ibsen, Chekhov, *et al.*—makes use of the melodramatic form but avoids its flaws. By adding depth to characterisation through descriptive detail, it avoids simplistic externalisations of conflict. Griffith and Borzage, like their literary predecessors, use and believe in the melodrama as a way of seeing the world, but also, by shifting their focus from the melodramatic situation itself to the *characters* in that situation, give the form depth and beauty. Griffith's and Borzage's whole-hearted commitment to a melodramatic world view, apparent in the intensity of feeling behind each shot in their films, invests their work with an emotional level that re-vitalises the melodramatic form and redeems the simplicity of the characters' struggle with their environment.

What distinguishes Borzage's melodramas from Griffith's is their spirituality. Where Griffith concerns himself primarily, like Dickens, with the restitution of the family unit or the creation of a new family-like unit, Borzage's interests lie chiefly in the salvation of his characters—his concern is not with external but with internal order. Where Griffith's characters contain irrepressible physical vitality—a vitality that makes the films immediate and direct—Borzage's characters, though also physical beings, radiate from within a unique, spiritual energy that makes them appear luminescently unreal.

Borzage's characters possess a strange, fascinating mixture of spiritual purity and physical attractiveness. Where Griffith tends to evoke either madonna-like innocence (Gish) or wholesome physicality (Dempster) in his characters, Borzage inextricably combines both these qualities (Farrell, Gaynor, Tracy, Young). But the sensuality of Borzage's character is rooted in their innocence and does not, as in DeMille, lead to their corruption. Rather, the purity of Borzage's sensuality reflects a total ignorance of the state of sin. The pre-lapsarian sensuality of his characters does not destroy but affirms their spirituality. Though a love relationship in Borzage often begins, as it does in *Street Angel* (1928), with physical attraction, the lovers ultimately go beyond their initial, mutual sexual desire to a more spiritual, quasi-religious awareness of and dependence on one another. Borzage's films concern themselves more with the exploration of the essences behind physical reality: unlike Griffith, Borzage attempts to deal purely with the souls of his characters.

The greatness of the ending of *Seventh Heaven,* for example, depends largely on a denial of physical reality in favour of a more ethereal one. When Chico (Charles Farrell) goes off to war, he and Diane (Janet Gaynor) promise to think of one another every day at eleven o'clock. During this mystical communication, Borzage cuts from one to the other as they repeat the words, "Chico . . . Diane . . . Heaven." Near the end of the war, Chico is wounded and dies in the arms of a priest. Diane, worried because Chico has not answered her at eleven for several days, gets the notification of Chico's death as the Armistice is signed and collapses. At that moment, as the clock begins to strike eleven, Borzage cuts to Chico, totally blind, struggling through the crowded streets below, trying to reach Diane and driven on by an inner vision. As Chico enters the apartment where Diane is waiting and falls at her feet, Borzage cuts to a high-angle, overhead shot of the lovers as they embrace.

Chico's miraculous return to life is no lapse in narrative continuity but an illustration of the transcendent nature of love in Borzage's work. Chico and Diane's love defies not only time and space but also mortality. The ending of *Seventh Heaven* destroys narrative logic and physical reality to reveal the strength of the spirit behind that reality and the existence of an eternal, abstract level of experience that mysteriously defies death itself.

SEVENTH HEAVEN: Chico (Charles Farrell) and Diane (Janet Gaynor)

STREET ANGEL

In the course of this article, I intend to examine the various forms Borzage's spirituality takes from film to film and to show how it relates to the director's use of traditional melodramatic form. The first few shots of *Street Angel*, perhaps the director's greatest silent film, describe this spirituality—the essences behind things—far better than words ever could. The first title of the film sets the mood: "Everywhere . . . in every town . . . in every street . . . we pass, unknowing, human souls made great by love and adversity." After this remarkably explicit title, Borzage's camera wanders through the dark, crowded streets of Naples. In the background of an expressionistic city set a man gets his shoes shined by a boy. Two policemen, making their rounds, meet. Borzage cuts to a circus troupe arguing with a vendor over a stolen sausage. A crowd gathers and the policemen arrive to settle the dispute. Then Borzage cuts to a tracking shot along the street: a priest walks down a stone stairway and the camera dollies in to a beggar girl sitting at the foot of the stairs, asking for alms. The camera continues to track past a man milking goats, past a fruit stand where a customer is haggling over a price with the fruit-seller, to a knot of women talking at the foot of a stairway in a courtyard. Borzage cuts to a shot of two women on the stairway, waiting to find out what's going on inside an apartment. Finally, he cuts into an apartment in which a doctor is telling Angela (Janet Gaynor) that she must buy some medicine in order to save her sick mother.

This opening establishes the film's atmosphere. Borzage creates a feel for the bustle of city life and suggests its cruel indifference to individual misfortune. Like the man who, later on in the opening sequence, calmly continues to eat his dinner, ignoring Angela's awkward solicitation, the details in the environment construct a world of separate, unconnected characters. By shooting the sequence and directing the actors as he does, Borzage captures a sense of discreet stories occurring in a continuous, all-encompassing environment. Though all the stories take place independently of one another, Borzage ties them all together into a single event by use of connective camera movement and editing. Though different and separate from one another, they share a common setting and atmosphere. This sort of thing makes no sense logically, as it would in Griffith, but it does work intuitively to define the indifference, sordidness and despair of the environment that begins the film.

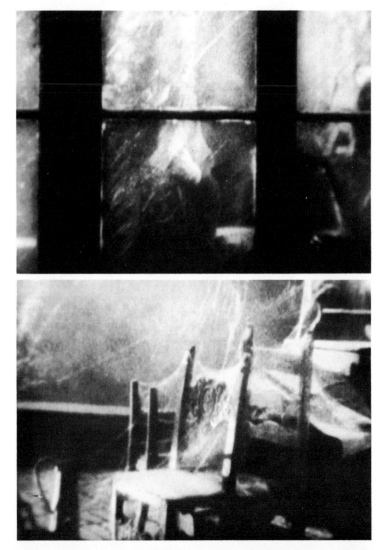

Borzage's expressionistic lighting and shooting style gives the environment a feeling of gloom that echoes the depression within his characters. The lighting and the cold, grey enormity of the studio sets create a dark, impersonal and physically and spiritually overwhelming world. The heavy mist that shrouds the action swallows up Angela's futile attempts to escape a world that makes her an orphan and threatens her with imprisonment. Arrested for robbery while "soliciting," Angela runs away as she is taken to prison. At home she finds her mother dead. Pursued by the police over rooftops and down darkly-lit streets, Angela is befriended by circus gypsies and leaves the city with them.

Angela meets Gino (Charles Farrell), an itinerant artist, and, in spite of her own cynicism, gradually falls in love with him. Gino joins the troupe and paints her portrait. When together they return to the city, they have one another to protect them from the city's cold impersonality. They build their own world and insulate it against external evils. Borzage's direction makes Gino's apartment a warm, intimate place—a bastion of innocence against the evil that surrounds them. The depravity of the outside world, personified in the prostitute Lisetta, works as a foil for the purity of Angela and Gino's love. Lisetta's yearning for Gino manifests itself as a pursuit of innocence: she wants his purity in order to corrupt it. Her failure to seduce Gino only magnifies the idyllic beauty of this love.

The threatening hostility of the world around them drives Borzage's lovers closer together and transforms their initial, physical attraction into a deeper, more spiritual love. Borzage uses Gino's portrait of Angela to represent the abstract, transcendent nature of this relationship. As Angela and Gino fall in love, Gino paints her portrait. His painting gives her an ethereal quality, showing her

Opposite: Angela (Janet Gaynor) outside Gino's empty apartment in STREET ANGELS (above): Gino's abandoned chair in the same film (below). Frame enlargements

not so much as she really is but as he sees her. In order to eat, they sell the painting to an art dealer. Yet even though it has been sold, the painting and its absence exert a powerful influence over the lovers. When Borzage cuts to shots of the bare wall where the painting was hung, the emptiness there conveys even more profoundly the painting's metaphysical significance: it, like their love, transcends material reality. Meanwhile, the art dealer, hoping to make a great deal of money on Gino's painting, hires another artist to re-touch it and to forge out of it an "Old Master." Several times during the film Borzage cuts back to the painting of Angela: as she herself becomes more and more completely changed by her love for Gino and her trials in the world, the painting is slowly transformed into a madonna. When Angela, without Gino's knowledge, is taken back to jail after spending her last hour with him, Borzage cuts to a shot of the forger painting a halo over her head.

Angela's disappearance and seeming desertion of him crushes Gino (who knew nothing of her arrest or past). He becomes disillusioned and bitter. When Angela is finally released, she searches for Gino but can't find him. Lisetta, who found Angela in jail, tells Gino that Angela was arrested for soliciting. He, believing that Angela has betrayed their love, decides to paint women as he now believes they really are—with the faces of angels but devils beneath —and goes out into the night in search of a model. Wandering the docks in a fog that reflects their mutual despair and resigned hopelessness, Angela and Gino meet. Looking as if he could kill her, Gino chases Angela through the fog into a church. He catches her and starts to strangle her on the altar when he accidentally knocks over a Bible, looks up and realises where he is. With his hands still around her throat, Gino lifts his eyes and sees his transformed painting of Angela hanging above the altar. Borzage here cuts to a high-angle shot of Gino and Angela *from the position of the painting*. Another cut shows the painting from Gino's point of view.

STREET ANGEL: Angela gazes hungrily at a plate of clams after her release from jail

After Borzage again cuts to a high-angle shot of Gino from the painting's standpoint, Gino releases his grip, moves backward and respectfully removes his hat. He glances from Angela to the portrait and says, "To think I once painted you like that . . ." Angela looks up at the painting, then at Gino and replies, "But I'm still like that. Look into my eyes." Gino looks into her eyes, sees her purity and innocence there and lifts her up off the floor. As they embrace, Borzage cuts to a final shot of the portrait which slowly dissolves into a long shot of Gino carrying Angela home through the fog.

Borzage's dramatic cutting in this last scene brings the painting to life and reveals an awareness of a reality greater than the mundane, physical world. The inanimate painting, whose fantastic presence is felt most powerfully in the shots taken from its standpoint, actually interacts with the characters—first preventing Gino from killing Angela, then becoming the agent of their reunion. Its unlikely presence here is less absurd coincidence than it is indicative of the mystical design of Borzage's universe.

The strange force that the painting exerts does not restore Angela and Gino to their original love, however. Rather, it elevates their relationship to a spiritually more transcendent level. The religious atmosphere, coupled with the painting's transformation into a madonna, makes clear the quasi-religious nature of their new awareness of and need for one another. Through the painting, each redeems the other. Borzage's great dissolve from the painting to them eloquently equates the rebirth of their love with a greater, more mysterious spiritual regeneration.

A FAREWELL TO ARMS

The spiritual quality of Borzage's love relationships is made all the more powerful by the narrative backgrounds against which they are set: the hostile environments of war and economic depression or both seem to threaten their happiness. *Seventh Heaven, Farewell to Arms* (1932), *A Man's Castle* (1933), *Little Man, What Now?* (1934), *Three Comrades* (1938), *The Mortal Storm* (1940), *Till We Meet Again* (1944) and *China Doll* (1958) all contain hostile backgrounds which Borzage's central characters ultimately surpass. Yet the often chaotic worlds that surround these characters are no more "real" in a physical sense than the characters themselves are. In other words, the backgrounds do not impose real or physical danger on the central characters; the chaos of the backgrounds is not a physical but a spiritual one.

A Farewell to Arms, based on Hemingway's novel, concerns the love affair of a soldier and a nurse who meet on the Italian front during the First World War. The film begins with a long shot of the beautiful Italian countryside, with the snowcapped Alps in the background. The camera pans left to a man lying in the foreground, smiling and seemingly asleep in this pastoral setting. But as the pan continues, it reveals that the man's leg has been blasted away and the man is not sleeping but dead. In the background of the shot, a caravan of medical trucks and ambulances slowly struggles up a steep mountain road, carrying wounded and dying soldiers. Cutting into this background, Borzage shows Lt. Frederick Henry (Gary Cooper), who is an Ambulance Corps officer, asleep in the front seat of an ambulance, carried along by the war but oblivious to it.

This opening sequence, contrasting the innocent beauty of the landscape with the grim horror and ugliness of war, establishes the basic situation of the film: characters, surrounded by war's bleakness and horror, surrender themselves to a protective pessimism that prevents them from really seeing that war and, at the same time, deadens their responses to one another. As the priest tells Lt. Henry later, he doesn't really see the war or feel it. In such an environment, love seems impossible. Alcohol and sex take its place, enabling characters to shut out the pain and death around them. Borzage begins a sequence with a line of troops marching from right to left outside a window shuttered with open venetian blinds. He slowly tracks back to a close-up of a woman's foot which the drunk Lt. Henry is playing with. The war in the background pervades the action in the foreground.

War and its spirit is constantly in the background, threatening and separating the lovers. When the lovers spend a night together, Borzage shows them, with a high-angle shot that cranes down on

87

A FAREWELL TO ARMS: Lt. Henry (Gary Cooper) joins his friend, Major Rinaldi (Adolph Menjou) in dissipation, to forget the horrors of war outside

them, outside under the statue of a rearing horse. Beneath its hoofs, the couple is simultaneously menaced and protected. At the end of the love scene, Borzage cuts back from Lt. Henry and nurse Barkley (Helen Hayes) to a shot of troops and trucks moving from right to left in the foreground, obscuring the lovers in the background.

On either side of the two lovers, Borzage positions bitterly pessimistic characters who try to discourage their friends from involvement in a serious love relationship. Rinaldi (Adolphe Menjou),

Henry's best friend, tells him, "Sacred subjects are not good for soldiers," and suggests, "Why don't you be like me—all fire and smoke and nothing inside." Catherine Barkley's friend, Fergie (Mary Phillips), fears almost insanely that her friend will be hurt by a war-doomed love affair and tries, as does Rinaldi, to separate the lovers. But neither war nor its agents can part them because of the spiritual purity of their union.

The spiritual threat of the chaotic environment that surrounds the lovers is most dramatically shown when Lt. Henry, deserting the Italian army—including his cynical friend Rinaldi—goes back to search for Catherine. Borzage surrounds him with death, destruction, explosions, and horrible human misery in the ranks of the wounded and retreating soldiers that culminates in the bombing of a graveyard. Henry's search for Catherine, set in the midst of all this spiritual bleakness, becomes a metaphorical journey and, because of the strength and explicitness of its image, the sequence emerges as one of the most powerfully direct thematic statements in the film.

At the end of the film, as Catherine is dying, Henry tells her that they will never be separated, even by her death. After she dies, Borzage cuts first to the Armistice celebration outside, then back to Lt. Henry as he picks Catherine up and, turning his back to the camera, carries her to the window. Looking out at the jubilation below, he mutters, "Peace . . . peace!" Borzage dissolves to a shot of pigeons flying to end the film. Peace ironically comes with the lovers' final transcendence of war. Though Catherine's tragic death finally releases the lovers from war's grip and unites them in an eternal, inseparable way, it also leaves Lt. Henry alone and lost with the new peace. One of Borzage's most moving conclusions, the ending of *Farewell to Arms* presents a paradox that reappears throughout the director's work: his characters achieve spiritual gain only through physical loss.

A MAN'S CASTLE

Man's Castle, one of Borzage's most romantic films, uses the American Depression as a melodramatic background for the central love relationship, but detaches its characters from the bleak reality of their historical setting. Unlike the physical oppressiveness of the anonymous environment surrounding King Vidor's characters in *The Crowd* (1928) or *Our Daily Bread* (1934), Borzage's depression setting is less a physical than a spiritual threat to his characters. What endangers Borzage's characters is not the depression's poverty or unemployment but, as in *Little Man, What Now?*, the spirit

MAN'S CASTLE: Bill (Spencer Tracy) exercises an absurd independence by becoming a walking bill-board. Frame enlargement

MAN'S CASTLE: Trina (Loretta Young) looking at a stove in a store window. Frame enlargement

of decadence and aimlessness with which it pervades them.

The plot of *Man's Castle* resembles that of *Seventh Heaven*. A man picks up a girl, takes her in, feeds, shelters and protects her while she gradually wins his love and gives him a new, more spiritual outlook on life. Unlike Charles Farrell's Chico, Spencer Tracy's Bill is a hard-boiled, tough, sceptical outsider who, though generous and kind, growls at everyone, preserving a gruff exterior that permits him to disengage himself from any deep commitment to the world around him. Bill's self-sufficiency and independence seem, at first, to be great strengths: he lives out in the open, uses his wits to obtain food and shelter and doesn't believe in regular jobs. His defiance of and detachment from the depression world represent his attempt to find a liberty that will enable him to escape the reality of his environment. Yet his carefree existence has its origins more in aimlessness than in any real sense of freedom. The promotional costumes Bill wears—the "Gilsey House Coffee" neon sign or the Gotham Eatery sandwich board—betray the falseness of his liberation from ordinary concerns and, like the grotesqueness of his clown-on-stilts outfit, reflect the absurdity of the freedom which his eccentricity and egoism have given him.

The logical extension of Bill's self-indulgent pursuit of freedom is loneliness and isolation. Though Bill's relationship with Trina (Loretta Young) offers him an alternative to this course, he stubbornly fights it, constantly drawn away from her by the sound of the train whistle, a symbol of his restless wanderlust.

The shack that Bill and Trina occupy comes to stand for the transitional, peaceful yet uncertain, state of their relationship. Though it is only a patchwork of old lumber, junk, old doors and windows, it is—through Trina's presence in it—their defence against the outside world. Trina calls it a "safety zone," a safe place in the street where pedestrians can stand until the cars go by. Structurally, it contains part of both their personalities. Trina's stabilising and ordering nature is seen in the stove, the curtains, the washboard and basin; Bill's quest for freedom appears in the sliding window in the ceiling that looks out on the blue sky and flying birds. Yet their shack, though its architecture foreshadows Bill and Trina's final union, is a structure that must be outgrown or transcended, like the drifting characters (e.g., Flossie, Bragg, Fay La Rue) around them, in order for Bill and Trina to realise freedom through love.

The movement in *Man's Castle,* as in countless other Borzage films, is towards the discovery that self-sufficient independence is weakness, not strength; and the acknowledgement that only through love or through a belief in something outside of oneself can people escape the cynicism and despair that threatens to destroy them. Bill's acknowledgement and acceptance of Trina's love frees them both from the fearful grip of the chaotic world around them. At the end of the film, Bill and Trina (pregnant with his child) hop a freight and set off to make a new start. Borzage's camera, in a movement that echoes their final spiritualisation and freedom, cranes up and away from them, as they lie together on the straw-covered floor of a boxcar. Detached from their restricting environment, they seem to float freely in space, triumphant and eternal in their love.

Sensuality of image in Borzage's films. Loretta Young as Trina in MAN'S CASTLE. Frame enlargement

LITTLE MAN, WHAT NOW?

Borzage's *Little Man, What Now?*, like Griffith's *Isn't Life Wonder-ful?* (1924), is set in the postwar depression of Twenties Germany and, like the Griffith film, treats the cold economic reality of that depression as if it were a villainous character in a melodrama. Griffith's direction portrays his characters' environment as a looming monster: when Hans (Neil Hamilton) and Inga (Carol Dempster) drag their precious cartload of potatoes homeward, the tall trees concealing their attackers in the surrounding woods dramatically overwhelm the lovers. Borzage's film also shows the depression melodramatically in terms of its effect on a young couple "all but submerged by the cruelties of the depression."* But, where Griffith uses the environment to physically threaten his characters, Borzage abstracts the forces that threaten his characters, concerning himself more with the spirit of depression than with its reality.

The film begins in the rain. Like the fog and mist in *Street Angel,* the weather here reflects a spiritual atmosphere, engulfing the characters in a gloomy, sunless world. The camera slowly dollies in on a knot of people standing in a park and listening to a radical's angry speech about injustice and inequality. Borzage dissolves to another dolly shot—a mirror image of the first—that tracks in on Hans Pinne-berg (Douglass Montgomery) standing alone in the street, waiting for Lämmchen (Margaret Sullavan) outside Dr. Sesam's office. The stylistic similarity of the introduction of Hans to that of the men in the street draws him, even though he's presented in a different and separate spatial matrix, into the discontent and bitterness of their outlook on life. Hans can't hear what the speaker is saying. When an old man tells him, he rejects the speaker's philosophy. Yet the parallel introduction draws him into the mob's mood of depression

---

* This phrase is excerpted from an article on *Little Man, What Now?* by Borzage that appears in the film's pressbook.

and their destructive pessimism, though externalised, becomes part of him, threatening to drown him.

When Lämmchen appears, the film comes to life. Borzage's startlingly exciting cuts to her in close-up—she seems to come out of nowhere—introduce us to an amazing source of positive energy, counterbalancing the negative forces around the couple. The abruptness of her close-up introduction, magnified by Margaret Sullavan's radiant expression, seems to jolt Hans out of his momentary despair. Later, at the doctor's, when Hans answers the nurse's questions about his parents by telling her that his father died of "war," he starts to drift away, apparently thinking about his father's death and the tragedies of the late war. Lämmchen's emergence from the doctor's office, like her first appearance, recalls him from his melancholic despondency. Lämmchen's mysteriously redemptive presence offsets the destructive forces of the rain, the men in the street and the depression that grew out of the past war. In the face of the problems that surround them, she embodies, literally (because of her pregnancy) and figuratively, new hope for the future.

Throughout the film, Borzage uses Lämmchen's innocence to counteract the cynicism that surrounds her and her husband. She serves as a spiritual beacon for Hans. Her three images, reflected in the mirrors of a dresser that Hans buys her, magnify and multiply her power. The reflections, shown as bright images that emanate from her, transform her, as she sits in front of her mirrors, into a source of light and strength. Borzage's treatment of Lämmchen— like the fantastic white dress she wears, made of scores of yards of lace and covered with iridescent sequins—makes her a romantic deity-figure through whom Hans finds redemption from the decadence of the other characters in his world. The pessimism of the voices that cry out in the streets in the rain-drenched opening sequence, of the angry man who paranoically blames "them" for his poverty, hunger, and, finally, for the death of his wife, offers Hans nothing but empty, bitter despair. Kleinholz, Hans's grotesque-looking employer, echoes the hollowness of the values represented by the film's minor characters: he hires only unmarried clerks to provide unwilling suitors for his plain, silly daughter, and fires Hans when, failing to corrupt him, he discovers Hans's secret marriage to Lämmchen. Moving to Berlin, Hans and Lämmchen find questionable refuge with Hans's step-mother, Mia Pinneberg, whose perverse relationship with her dog and wild, degenerate parties mirror the larger, all-consuming depravity that she and her world represent for the young couple.

It is the cynicism and negative quality of these characters that threaten Hans and Lämmchen, not the physical fact of economic depression. Only Lämmchen's radiant presence gives Hans the strength and courage to transcend his bleak environment. The birth of their child at the end of the film—the infant, like Lämmchen earlier, is shown in soft, ethereal close-ups—symbolises their triumph over life's negativity through their creation of a new, pure, positive being whose redemptive power lies in the fact that it is nothing but life itself.

*   *   *

A majority of the best films Borzage made in the late Twenties and early Thirties depend for their success on the creation of a pair of great screen lovers. As Andrew Sarris writes, "Frank Borzage was that rarity of rarities, an uncompromising romanticist." One of the great virtues of his early films lies in his ability to convey "the wondrous inner life of lovers in the midst of adversity."* Each of Borzage's films reveals a profound commitment to the love story not only as something with a life of its own but as a dramatic parable that hymns the power of love. *Seventh Heaven, Street Angel, A Farewell to Arms, A Man's Castle,* and *Little Man, What Now?* are

---

* Andrew Sarris, *The American Cinema,* New York: E. P. Dutton & Co., 1968, p. 86.

all variations on a single romantic theme: two lovers, adrift on a stormy sea of war or economic depression, find, through their love, calm weather and a provident, following wind that carries them to a safe harbour. The positive optimism of Borzage's work as a whole rests on a deeply felt belief in love as a redemptive force. In film after film, he presents a couple, reveals that one or both have fallen (in the Miltonic sense of the word) into seemingly incurable melancholia, bitterness or despair, then oversees his characters' restoration to an edenic state of innocence through the purity of their love. This pattern appears, with varying degrees of explicitness, in almost all his work, even in his minor films. In *Stranded* (1935), Lynn Palmer (Kay Francis), one of Borzage's more allegorical characters, works for Traveler's Aid, guiding lost or confused people to their destination. When she meets and falls in love with a tough, doggedly inflexible engineer (George Brent) who is building a bridge, she helps him outgrow the cynical egotism and blind, hardheaded independence which interferes with his love for her and with his work. The therapeutic and redemptive nature of Borzage's love relationships gives his films a quasi-religious quality. As a result, though his early films are primarily romantic in outlook, many of them contain religious elements. *Seventh Heaven* uses a religious miracle to re-unite its lovers at the end. The final scene of *Street Angel* takes place in a church and involves Angela's transfiguration, paralleling that of her portrait, into a madonna. *Man's Castle* ends with Bill and Trina in a boxcar manger, projecting the birth of their child for Christmas.

In the latter part of the Thirties, the content of Borzage's films changes, becoming more overtly religious. Starting with *Green Light* (1937) and culminating in *Strange Cargo* (1940), Borzage shifts the dramatic focus of his films from the central love relationship to a more general concern for the spiritual well-being of not only his lovers but other characters around them. *Green Light* and

Disputed Passage (1939), both based on Lloyd C. Douglas novels, follow the gradual conversion of agnostic doctors to a belief in something outside of themselves, to a discovery that, through sacrifice, they can become part of a redemptive, spiritual system. In *Green Light,* Dr. Paige (Errol Flynn), assuming the responsibility for a patient's death, sacrifices his career and risks his life experimenting with a serum to combat spotted fever. Inspired by the religious stoicism of Mrs. Dexter (the dead patient) and by the words of Dean Harcourt (Mrs. Dexter's religious preceptor), Paige works out his own redemption when he experiments on himself in order to save a small Montana community plagued by the fever. Paige's suffering and sacrifice purify not only himself but also Phyllis Dexter (Anita Louise), the dead patient's bitter daughter who both loves and hates Paige; Dr. Endicott whose carelessness led to Mrs. Dexter's death; and nurse Ogilvie (Margaret Lindsay) who vainly loves Paige and tries to help him by revealing Endicott's culpability in the Dexter case. Similarly, in *Disputed Passage,* the scientific scepticism of Dr. Beaven (John Howard) crumbles when it confronts the religious mysticism of Audrey Hilton (Dorothy Lamour), one of his patients.° He eventually follows her to China. When Beaven stops his search for her to aid a bombed-out Chinese village, he becomes wounded himself, struck on the head while rescuing a crippled child from a collapsing hospital during an air raid. As he lies unconscious, the missionary doctor, Dr. La Ferriere, sends for Dr. Forster (Akim Tamiroff), Beaven's cynical professor and the man who prevented Beaven's marriage to Audrey. Forster arrives and operates, saving his student's life, but Beaven, having lost the will to live, remains unconscious. It is only with Audrey's arrival that Beaven comes out of his coma, literally recalled to life

---

°Fred Camper's article on *Disputed Passage* in "Cinema" (U.K.) no. 9 is the best discussion of the film I have seen and one of the best pieces on Borzage in general.

by her. Even the dubious Dr. Forster is drawn into the mystical, spiritual regeneration that Beaven's recovery creates. In both films, each character's salvation is inextricably bound up with those of the other characters and the regeneration of one mysteriously leads to the regeneration of all.

Though *Three Comrades* (1938) and *The Shining Hour* (1938) have a stronger romantic base than either *Green Light* or *Disputed Passage,* the overall thrust of the later films is away from specific romantic concerns and toward the more general, spiritual awakening of the Douglas doctor films. In *Three Comrades,* the love relationship between Erich (Robert Taylor) and Pat (Margaret Sullavan) is interwoven with the loyalty and friendship of the lovers with Otto (Franchot Tone) and Gottfried (Robert Young), Erich's war comrades. Gottfried's death, Otto's sacrifices and Pat's sacrificial death at the end transform the four-way relationship into a complex affinity between the living and the dead and deal with feelings that go beyond time and space. Like *Three Comrades, The Shining Hour* is not about religion, yet is deeply religious in its treatment of romantic relationships. The plot of the film is turgidly melodramatic. When a Wisconsin dairy-farmer, Henry Linden (Melvyn Douglas), asks a sophisticated Manhattan showgirl, Olivia Riley (Joan Crawford), to marry him, Henry's brother David (Robert Young) flies to New York to try to stop him. Unable to prevent the marriage, David becomes attracted to Olivia. At the wedding, Borzage cuts quickly from close-ups of Henry to Olivia to David and, finally, back to Olivia, extending the marriage bond to a three-way union that continues until the closing moments of the film. Later, in Wisconsin, when David grows more deeply in love with Olivia, Judy (Margaret Sullavan), David's devoted wife, tells Olivia that David never really loved her (Judy). Olivia admits that she never told Henry that she loved him. As the two talk, Borzage's close-up cutting binds the women together into a strangely sympathetic alliance. For the sake of David's happiness, Judy asks Olivia to run away with him. Later, during a fire set by Hanna (Fay Bainter), David and Henry's neurotically protective sister, that destroys Henry and Olivia's new home, Judy dashes into the flames in an attempt to sacrifice herself and clear the way for David and Olivia. Olivia follows her into the fire and rescues her. The next day, in one of Borzage's most moving sequences, Olivia oversees the reconciliation of Judy, her face covered with bandages, and David, then leaves the Linden farm only to be pursued by her husband Henry.

The series of multiple sacrifices that concludes *The Shining Hour* changes its characters' petty, superficial, self-indulgent romantic longings into a more genuine, deeply-felt, quasi-religious awareness. Its characters, through their sacrifices and sufferings, attain a spiritual purity that enables them to respond more honestly and directly to one another than ever before. What makes *The Shining Hour* so moving and different from Borzage's earlier work is that all its major characters—even the villainous Hanna—take part in a spiritual awakening and that each character's new sensitivity to his world is magnified by and echoed in each succeeding character's spiritual re-birth.

STRANGE CARGO

The deeper commitment to religious concerns that began with *Green Light* finds its greatest expression in *Strange Cargo,* perhaps Borzage's most explicit film. *Strange Cargo* begins in a penal colony in the French Guianas. An overhead shot introduces us, in long shot, to files of anonymous prisoners lifelessly marching through a bright, sunlit prison yard. Moments later, the first shot of Verne (Clark Gable), one of the film's central characters, shows him emerging, alone, from the dark shadows of a solitary confinement cell and seemingly wrestling (or so his hand gestures suggest) with the unaccustomed light. Verne's introduction—his release and entry into the light—prefigures his spiritual evolution through the course of the film. Yet it also, in contrast to the introduction of the exhausted ranks of prisoners in the yard, reveals Verne's great strength and raw physical energy: his determination to escape and his independence give him a vitality, like that of Bill in *Man's Castle*, that the other prisoners lack. In the midst of the deadness that surrounds him, he remains full of life. When he sees Julie (Joan Crawford) for the first time, Verne responds sexually to her. On the dock, when she throws away a cigarette, he grabs it. He first sniffs the lipstick on the cigarette, tastes it, then smokes it more as if he were kissing Julie than smoking her cigarette. Later, he grabs Julie's ankle and refuses to let her go until he has made a date with her. His sexual response to her characterises the physicality of their relationship, yet provides a basis for the transition to a deeper, more romantic involvement. When Verne tenderly reads her a quasi-erotic passage from "The Song of Solomon,"—"Behold thou art fair, my love . . ." —his earlier, crude, physical attraction to her seems to deepen into an emotional engagement with her as a romantic figure.

Borzage integrates the love relationship between Verne and Julie into a larger system of relationships. Though their love serves as a dramatic focus in the film, the actual agent of Verne and Julie's transformation is not only their love but also Cambreau (Ian Hunter), a mysterious figure whose omniscience, omnipotence and omnipresence oversee each character's regeneration. Cambreau functions as a sort of catalyst, controlling the characters and bringing them to a new spiritual state. Guided by Cambreau, Borzage's characters —both the escaped convicts and the exiled Julie—embark on a journey to the mainland that becomes a metaphor for their trek towards spiritual liberation. Though they escape the physical confines of the prison, nature itself becomes an obstacle to their search for freedom.

They spend one-third of the picture wandering through dense jungle or swamp and another third adrift in a small sailboat, without drinking water, on a windless sea. As the escaping convicts die one by one of hunger, thirst, snakebite, sharks, etc., Cambreau's presence enables them to accept their own mortality and to understand their own divinity. He converts them to a spiritual system that helps them realise their quest for freedom.

The jungle and the sea—elements which the characters try to master—become an extension of Cambreau, providing the characters with an adversity to which, like Cambreau's spirituality, they eventually yield. Cambreau's seeming control over nature, the sureness with which he finds trails in the jungle or the accuracy with which he predicts the becalming of the sea, suggests a supernatural awareness and reflects his strange identification with the natural world. Cambreau's introduction to and exit from the film reveal his oneness with the environment: he mysteriously enters out of the background to take Verne's place in line at the prison gate and, with equal mystery, vanishes into the background at the end of the film. Like the fisherman who shares the last shot of the film with him, Cambreau is at ease with nature. Both he and the fisherman (who crosses himself as Cambreau exits) seem to share a sublime knowledge and grace that reveal their simultaneous transcendence of and union with the world around them. Cambreau's inseparability from the world around him transforms the natural background—the prison, jungle, swamp, sea—into a part of his spiritual system, into a divine agent against which Borzage's characters struggle in vain. The tempestuous rain and stormy sea at the end of the film, for example, provide Verne with the opportunity of saving himself by saving Cambreau. After a fight with Cambreau, Verne throws him overboard to drown. He taunts Cambreau, telling him that, "I'm the only one who can save you now." He shouts out, "I'm God," and as he's about to say, "You're God," lightning flashes overhead; Verne suddenly understands the divinity of life itself, realises that Cambreau *is* God, dives into the sea and rescues him.

Verne's discovery of a need for something outside of himself, though centrally at issue in his relationship with Cambreau and his spiritual system, leads him to a deeper love of and need for Julie. What is great about *Strange Cargo* is the interdependence of these two threads. Borzage's demand that his characters attain a spiritual awareness that goes beyond an immediate love relationship to a sympathy with and need for the world around them marks a significant expansion of the director's concerns and a deepening of the beauty of his art.

THE MORTAL STORM

The Mortal Storm, Borzage's next film, interweaves a love story with the greater emotional and spiritual vicissitudes of a family and (by extension) a nation, going even further than *Strange Cargo* in its concern for its characters' salvation. Set against the background of Germany on the eve of Hitler's appointment to the post of chancellor, *The Mortal Storm* presents a world that slowly and surely disintegrates around its characters, leaving them nothing but memories and shadows in an empty house.

The film opens with a prologue narration: time-lapse photography shows a grey sky filled with clouds that rapidly gather and move in the wind. The narrator talks about primitive man's search for shelter against the wind, rain, thunder and lightning and speaks of "the mortal storm in which man finds himself today." More important, however, than the narrator's melodramatic words are the cosmic images that accompany them for they convey a feeling for the presence of unknown, supernatural forces at work in the universe. As a result of the prologue, these unseen forces, more than

THE MORTAL STORM: Freya (Margaret Sullavan) and Martin (James Stewart) watch the world around them slowly Nazify. Frame enlargement

the characters and melodrama that follow, become the subject of Borzage's film.

After the prologue, Borzage begins the film's narrative with an establishing long shot of the snow-capped mountains that surround the Roths' village. Through the course of the film, we see that Borzage's central characters, Professor Roth (Frank Morgan) and his wife, his daughter Freya (Margaret Sullavan), his student Martin (James Stewart) and Martin's mother (Maria Ouspenskaya) stand, like these mountains, eternal and fixed in their spiritual purity and strength within a rapidly changing, spiritually corrupt society.

When Professor Roth's step-sons, Otto (Robert Stack) and Erich (William T. Orr), and his best student, Fritz (Robert Young), reveal their conversion to Fascism at the professor's birthday party, Borzage illustrates their desertion of the professor's spiritual values through their departure from his table. When a maid enters with the announcement that Hitler has been appointed chancellor, Fritz, Otto, Erich and Rudi (the professor's youngest son) jump up from the table in their excitement and gather around the radio in the next room, listening to the news. Martin, Freya, the professor and his wife remain silent, sitting dejected at the half-empty table. When the others return, they stand around the table, again grouped differently from the professor's group. Borzage's editing here, first isolating, then grouping various characters together according to their beliefs, transforms the family from one based originally on ties of blood to one based on a more abstract, yet stronger bond of mutuality and affinity of spirit.

The family seems to crumble around the professor, yet the solidity of those who remain gives birth to a new alliance of souls. The two-shots of Martin and Freya, especially, create an unbreakable bond between them that, like the surrounding mountains, remains invulnerable to time and the transitory evils of a Fascist society.

Through a series of repeated shots and mirroring sequences, Borzage's visual style documents the transformation of the world around his characters. In *I've Always Loved You* (1946), Borzage's camera movements during Myra's second concert echo those during her first concert, given in the same place years earlier. By shooting the concerts in the same way, Borzage reveals that, in spite of outward changes in appearance, time and circumstance, his characters have not changed inwardly. Similarly, in *The Mortal Storm*, Borzage's repeated shots re-affirm the inner constancy of his characters' spirituality in the context of an altered environment. Borzage twice follows

Professor Roth to the university. Each time the camera tracks along-side him as he walks down a pillared entrance, shows him with his colleagues and his students. The first time, he arrives and is greeted respectfully by his friends and students. On this occasion, the school celebrates his birthday with the stamping of feet, speeches and the presentation of an award that symbolises the university's indebtedness to him—a statue of a figure with a torch, representing the knowledge that the professor passes on to his students. Later, when Borzage for the second time shows the professor's arrival, the university has been Nazified. Students and colleagues turn away from him, as an anti-Fascist and a Jew, and refuse to acknowledge his greetings. In class, his uniformed students challenge his facts about blood composition and walk out on him. Later, he observes, from his window, their book-burning ceremony, a reversal of his birthday celebration which transforms the earlier torch of learning into a bonfire of ignorance, cynicism and hate. Yet the professor holds fast to his beliefs, even in the gloomy darkness of the concentration camp to which he is sent and, by so doing, counterpoints the insanity of the world around him.

Again, when Freya brings Martin to a country inn for a re-union with his old friends, now Nazi converts, Borzage tracks through the inn, from right to left, to Freya and Martin's table as the people in the inn sing a pleasant drinking song. When some Nazi officials enter and lead the people in a martial song glorifying Fascism, Martin and Freya appear bewildered and ashamed, look-ing at the people saluting and singing around them. Borzage's camera slowly tracks, from left to right this time, back to the front of the inn, reversing the earlier movement and revealing the people in the inn transformed by the spirit of Fascism.

Borzage's use of repeated shots and sequences isolates his char-acters in a spiritually suffocating environment and alienates them from its corruptness. Borzage's alignment of characters under opposing systems of belief reduces his melodrama to a conflict not so much between characters as between spiritual outlooks. Though one system seems to overwhelm the other—the professor dies in a concentration camp, Mrs. Roth and Rudi flee to Austria, Freya tries to escape from Germany with Martin but is shot by Fritz's men and dies in Martin's arms on the border—the grotesque brutality and spiritual barbarism of that system take their toll on those who try to adhere to it. In the last few shots of the film, Borzage re-affirms the transcendency of the eternal, cosmic forces associated with the professor's spiritual outlook over the corrupt system that opposes it. Otto and Erich visit their now-empty home and stand at a window watching the snow fall outside. Fritz enters and tells them of Freya's death. After Fritz's exit, Erich speaks angrily of Martin's escape and remarks bitterly, "He's free." Otto replies, "Yes. Free to think as he chooses." Erich corrects his brother, "Free to fight against everything we believe in." Otto answers back, "Yes. Thank God for that!" Erich, remaining dogmatic in his Fascist beliefs, slaps Otto and walks out. Otto, transformed by what he sees and what he has learned, walks about the empty house. Borzage's tracking camera shows us what he sees and suggests what he remembers: it tracks from Otto's face through an empty room to the dining room table. It looks where Freya used to sit and we hear her voice on the soundtrack, repeating what she said at the professor's birthday party. The camera angle changes to reveal the professor's empty chair, then goes past the chair to the shadow it casts on the floor as the professor also speaks. Borzage pans up to Martin's seat, accompanied by a reprise of Martin's refusal to convert to Fascism. Dollying-out into the hallway, the camera fixes on the shadow of the professor's torch-of-knowledge statue and the soundtrack recalls his speech when the statue was given to him. Borzage tracks past the statue itself and, as we hear Otto walk out and the door slam behind him, the camera swings around to look at the deserted hallway.

After a few seconds inside the empty house, Borzage cuts to a shot outside the Roth's gate that looks up their sidewalk at the house. As the camera pans down to the ground, we see Otto's footprints slowly fill in with new-fallen snow and vanish before our eyes.

The power and the beauty of this ending, like that of *A Farewell to Arms* in which Lt. Henry holds his dead "wife" in his arms as peace is announced, lies in the complexity of feelings it evokes. The disillusionment of Otto with the rigid Nazi dogma that has destroyed his family suggests his conversion to a more transcendent philosophy. Yet the cost at which this conversion comes, the loss of all that once had meaning for him, qualifies the triumph of his transformation.

The shots at the end that recall the professor's birthday party work, like the repeated shots described above, to emphasise the eternal and timeless nature of the professor's, Martin's and Freya's beliefs. At the same time, Otto's presence in the sequence draws him into Borzage's transcendent re-creation of the Roth family, linking him with their re-birth as spiritual forces. The snow outside that fills in Otto's footprints represents, in its purity and whiteness, not only his re-generation but also the larger triumph of eternal spirit over the transitory and ephemeral actions of individual men.* Though it erases the facts—i.e., footprints—of Otto's physical presence, it also integrates him with the invisible, immortal, cosmic forces that dominate the mortal storm in which man repeatedly finds himself. The film's cloud-filled prologue and snow-filled conclusion look away from the lesser reality of specific characters and events towards a greater, more abstract reality of the divine presence that animates the natural world and gives meaning to its inhabitants.

---

* The image, when Freya is shot escaping, of her blood on the snow reveals the outrageous barbarism of Fritz's action, yet prepares us for her union with eternal elements upon her death.

TILL WE MEET AGAIN

The gradual spiritualisation of Borzage's earlier, Thirties romanticism results in *Till We Meet Again,* a film at the heart of which lies a beautiful religious-romantic relationship between a nun and an aviator. Their attraction, though never explicitly realised in a love relationship (since the nun is married to her religion and the flier has a wife), gives the couple a platonically romantic union that enables their souls to bridge the gulfs that separate them. What makes the film work as well as it does is Borzage's ability to create an individual and particular relationship between his "lovers," yet also to make that relationship symbolise the larger interdependency of the two different worlds each character represents.

The action of the film is set against the grim background of occupied France during the Second World War. Like *A Farewell to Arms, Till We Meet Again* begins with shots of a placidly beautiful and peaceful landscape on which the war brutally intrudes. The film opens with a high-angle, crane shot that overlooks a small village and tracks slowly past a ringing bell in a church tower. The camera then moves alongside a double-file of children, all in white, following a nun through the convent grounds. White pigeons take flight as the group passes and a gardener respectfully takes off his hat. The nun, Sister Clothilde (Barbara Britton), stops the children near a garden well and begins a litany, praying aloud: "Have mercy on us . . ." and "Pray for us . . ." There is some noise off-screen. Borzage cuts to its source—a double-file of men, darkly dressed, guarded by Nazi soldiers, are being led off to German prison camps. Three men break rank and escape as the sentries fire after them. Borzage cuts back to Sister Clothilde vainly trying to drown out, through prayer, the gunshots she hears off-screen. After the litany, a child asks her, "What was that noise, Sister Clothilde?" She replies, "I don't know . . . I don't want to know."

Borzage's dramatic opposition of the two groups, the column of

109

children in white and the troop of men in dark clothes, visualises the film's central conflict between the interior world of the convent and the external world of war. Sister Clothilde's fear of the outside world, though partially justifiable, becomes a barrier to her achievement of spiritual maturity, to her coming to terms with the world. Her attempts to shut the world out of the convent fail. The war breaks in on her again and again—first, in the person of Major Krupp whose Nazi uniform and heavy, military boots awkwardly violate the convent's religious atmosphere and, then, with the entry of the American aviator, John (Ray Milland), through a trap door in a chapel basement. Believing that involvement with him and his world threatens her spiritual purity, Clothilde literally turns away from John: she stands in the dark chapel with her back to him. Though Clothilde tries melodramatically to externalise the forces of evil and to locate them solely in the outside world, Borzage, going beyond the limited vision of any one of his characters, undercuts the authority of the novice's self-confidence and untested surety in her faith by using the outside world to make trial of her religious beliefs.

Borzage counterbalances Sister Clothilde's awkward fear with the Mother Superior's calm control: Clothilde panics (e.g., Borzage shows a ball of yarn falling off her lap when she stands up to show her fright) when Major Krupp enters the convent and, in an attempt to protect one of her charges, betrays the aviator; the other deals easily with both the demands of the convent and the intrusion of the outside world. The Mother Superior's polite formality and verbal wit enable her to handle Major Krupp, and the active (as opposed to contemplative) nature of her faith prompts her to take part in the French Resistance, helping its members to escape the Nazis. Clothilde's awareness of her betrayal draws her closer to the Mother Superior's omniscient, experienced saintliness. In one sequence that prefigures Clothilde's subsequent identification with the Mother

110

Superior, Borzage's cuts place Clothilde in the same position in the frame that the Mother Superior occupies in the preceding and succeeding shots, welding them, through fusion of image, into a single, spiritual entity. And in the next scene, the Germans, searching for the aviator, shoot through the convent door, accidentally killing the Mother Superior. As she dies, the camera slowly cranes upward from her (with Clothilde at her side) to the ceiling, echoing the ascension of her spirit. The Mother Superior's death and Clothilde's guilt over her earlier betrayal force her into the outside world: she guides the downed pilot through enemy lines to the coast. Clothilde's accidental, although fortunate, death at the end of the film—an outgrowth of her resistance work—heralds her spiritual re-birth and further integrates her into the Mother Superior's transcendent spiritual system. With an overhead shot that stylistically recalls the Mother Superior's death, Borzage ties Clothilde's death to the earlier one and reaffirms the timeless nature of the spiritual order to which the two women belong.

Clothilde's entry into the outside world as the aviator's guide launches her on a journey much like that made by the characters in *Strange Cargo*. Symbolised by the moment in which she sees herself for the first time in a mirror, Clothilde's initiation into the real world leads her to discoveries not only about others (e.g. John's quasi-sacred ideas about marriage, his ability to show her that God is everywhere in the world) but also about herself. Through her pretended "marriage" to John and their night together in a rustic cottage, she attains an understanding of secular spirituality. Through John's escape at the end (through a trap door that recalls his first appearance), she realises her own spiritual freedom and re-dedicates herself to a life of service and sacrifice. As Borzage shows, Clothilde's earlier, cloistered saintliness robs her spirituality of meaning because she has only *escaped* not *transcended* the outside world. Her contact with that world, with the aviator and his system of values in particular, deepens her faith and leads her to a more profound understanding of what religion really is. Clothilde's crucifixion (when she dies, the camera pans to the cross in her hand) at the end of the film, representing her conversion to a more complex idea of spirituality, marks her transcendence of both the outside world and the cloister and her emergence into the deathless and eternal realm of pure spirit.

MOONRISE

Moonrise (1949) is probably Borzage's best-known and most universally admired sound film. In many ways, it is unlike any of his earlier works. Its plot, dealing with murder and guilt, departs dramatically from the simple love stories the director usually tells, and its heavily psychological approach to action and characterisation seems unusual for a director who concerns himself more with the soul and heart than with the mind. Stylistically, *Moonrise* marks a visual revolution of sorts for Borzage, with its tremendously dynamic compositions, tight framing and low-key lighting. The psychological intensity of Borzage's images, seen in his constant use of foreground-background interaction, rack focus, tight close-ups of parts of bodies (especially feet and hands), shadows and off-axis, angled shooting, seems to weigh oppressively on the film's characters, to constrict their actions and to prevent their spiritual liberation from the crazy forces that imprison them. Yet even though *Moonrise* looks different from Borzage's other work, it reveals as deep a commitment as ever to the concerns that occupy his other films.

The film begins with a nightmarish sequence showing the execution of Danny Hawkins's father for murder. Close-up tracking shots of legs walking towards the scaffold and shadows projected against the wall present the hanging indirectly. As a result, the execution seems much more traumatic. The shadows take on a supernatural quality, becoming demonic, deathless presences that, like the shadows on the wall of Plato's cave, have a ghostly, abstract reality of their own, a reality ultimately independent of the concrete reality of their source. As the trap springs, hanging Danny's father, Borzage cuts from a shadow of the execution to that of a doll suspended by a string over a baby's crib, transferring the spirits conjured up in the first scene into the next where they haunt the dead man's son. Borzage then intercuts a time montage of Danny's growth, seen in the tortures and torments of the boy's schoolmates, with a reprise of the original execution of his father, visualising the mystical control of the past over the present. In one shot, Borzage's vertiginous, high-angle long shot pins the boy down as he is taunted in a schoolyard: the camera's overhead position pushes down on Danny with all the weight of the previous action. At the end of the sequence, Borzage focuses on Danny's (Dane Clark) legs, as it earlier did his father's, walking through the woods towards his own spiritual "execution": he accidentally kills Jerry Sykes, his chief tormentor, and tries to conceal the crime. The forces of the past seem to possess Danny, driving his every movement and gesture, directing his feet in his father's footsteps. Only by freeing himself from these insane, disembodied spirits can Danny find peace for himself and begin to live his own life.

After the murder, Danny's irrational outbursts of violence and recklessness estrange him from the characters around him. He forces himself upon Gilly (Gail Russell), Sykes's girl, and almost kills her and another couple in a car crash. He turns away from his aunt in the next scene and even starts to withdraw from Gilly, who falls in love with him. Danny's guilt and fear of the past wall him up within himself. Like Billy Scripture (Henry Morgan), a deaf and dumb character with the mind of a child, Danny remains an outcast, shut off from the world around him. When Billy looks at

MOONRISE: Danny (Dane Clark) re-joins the human race by giving himself up to the sheriff (Allyn Joslyn)

the cement footprints he made in a sidewalk when he was a child, he tries to step in them and can't understand why his feet no longer fit them. Both he and Danny are prisoners of the past, locked in a frozen relationship with it. Though they change on the outside as time passes, they remain the same within and are powerless to come to terms with themselves as they are in the present.

Much of the overwhelming tenseness of the film grows out of Danny's rigid self-containment which walls him off from the characters who try to help him. Danny, like the old railroad brakesman

Mose (Rex Ingram), stands apart from the real world, withdrawn into one of his own creation. But where Mose's isolation represents a transcendence of the real world, Danny's rejection of those around him locks himself up in the prison of his own fear and hatred. Shot after shot in the film seems to trap Danny in a part of the frame. In the hardware store when Jerry's body is brought into town, Borzage pulls focus from the sheriff looking out the window in the background to Danny as he steps into the shot in the near foreground. The sudden focal change shifts all the pressure onto Danny, alone in the foreground. Through his relationship with Gilly, Danny finds moments of release from his self-imposed imprisonment. Because of his fear, they meet secretly at an old, abandoned plantation called Blackwater on the edge of a swamp. When Gilly pretends they're living in an earlier era—the pre-Civil War period of the room's *décor,* she and Danny dance. As they move through the room, the camera cranes up from them to the ceiling chandelier and floats weightlessly with them, momentarily freeing them both from time and space and transforming them into ethereal, romantic shapes. The camera cranes back down on them as they kiss, silhouetted against a lace-curtained window. Their lyrical metamorphosis into shadowy forms shatters the tenseness of their earlier encounters as separate individuals and draws them together into a single entity detached from time and free, for an instant, from their problems and the fears that divide them.

However, the private, romantic world they create for themselves does not last. At the county fair, for example, their earlier tenseness returns. Fearing the sheriff will see him with Gilly and suspect him of the Sykes murder, Danny drags Gilly through the crowds, pushing past people to an escape on the ferris wheel ride. Danny watches the sheriff and his wife get on the wheel below him and suddenly the ferris wheel itself becomes a circular prison. Danny breaks under the claustrophobic pressure that his guilt and fears produce, gets out of his seat and jumps from the top of the wheel to the ground.

Later, pursued by the sheriff and Mose's bloodhounds, Danny takes to the swamp. He seems to stumble blindly in no particular direction, chased more by his own fears than by the sheriff and his posse. Danny's flight and search for freedom takes him back into the past, to his grandmother's house in the hills and to his parents' graves. Only by coming to terms with the past that haunts him can Danny free himself from his isolation in the present and his claustrophobic self-containment. Near the end of the film, as Danny stands

CHINA DOLL: the daughter of Cliff and Shu-Jen identifies herself at the airport by showing her guardians Cliff's dog tags. Frame enlargement

over his parents' graves and lays his rifle down, Borzage cuts to a low-angle shot that places Danny against the bright, open sky behind him, suggesting the boy's liberation from the past by releasing him from the dark-edged, heavy, claustrophobic frames that have surrounded him throughout the film.

When Danny goes back to give himself up, Borzage literally shows him "rejoining the human race." In shots drenched with light, Danny hugs one of Mose's hunting dogs that was tracking him and stands waiting for the sheriff and his men. While he talks with the sheriff, he sees Gilly emerge from the woods. As she moves towards him, he starts to walk towards her and Borzage cuts from one to the other. The intercut tracking shots melt the movement of Danny walking towards Gilly with that of her walking towards him, reducing the space between the lovers. At the same time, the editing gives the pair an equality of weight, making Gilly not so much the means to Danny's redemption as his reward for it. Finally, once and for all, Danny's self-imposed isolation breaks down, and the scene mystically integrates him with Gilly in a timeless and weightless romantic union.

CHINA DOLL

Borzage's post-war films, though still concerned with religious and romantic issues, present characters blinded to happiness more by self-destructive forces within themselves than by the hostility of their environment. Their salvation necessitates an almost mystical, ritualistic re-enactment of an earlier, crippling incident through which they exorcise the spirits that haunt them. In *I've Always Loved You*, Myra can only free herself from Goronoff's mysterious grip by returning to Carnegie Hall and playing her concerto with him as she had years ago. In *That's My Man* (1947), Ronnie can win back and redeem Joe only by bringing Gallant Man—who symbolises their union—out of retirement to race again. Gallant Man's

117

exciting and moving come-from-behind victory heralds not only his but the lovers' rejuvenation. And in *Moonrise*, Danny's journey into the past literally lays to rest, as he puts down his rifle on his father's grave, the spirits that possessed him from the film's first traumatic scene.

The therapeutic revival of these postwar Borzage characters is less a matter of modern-day psychology than of primitive mysticism, their re-birth marking an initiation, with a new identity, into a transcendent spiritual system. *China Doll* (1959), Borzage's next-to-last film, also deals with a curative exorcism of the dark, destructive spirits that block its central character's realisation of happiness, but does so in a different and even more profoundly moving way than these earlier works do.

China Doll begins with a shot of an aeroplane flying through a clouded sky. Like the openings of *Living on Velvet* (1935) and *The Shining Hour*, the first shots of *China Doll* give a sense of characters floating aimlessly in space, without a specific destination or direction. Set in China during the Second World War, the film tells the story of a transport pilot, Cliff Brandon (Victor Mature), whose bitterness and cynicism, apparently results of the war, alienate him from his men and slowly destroy his soul. Brandon's loneliness and drifting purposelessness are not limited to his flights over China in the air. On the ground, he spends his time getting drunk at Sadie's place, a dingy, back-alley bar frequented by servicemen and prostitutes. When Brandon's flight crew enters the place, they see him sitting alone, drinking at the bar. Borzage's composition isolates him alone in the background, setting him apart from the camaraderie of his men in the foreground. One crew member points at him and asks, "What's he trying to drown?" Foster (Don Barry), Brandon's flight chief, explains: "Out here, you spend the first four months of your duty catching up on your reading, the second four catching up on women and the next four catching up on your drinking."

Like Joe Grange's gambling fever in *That's My Man*, Brandon's drunkenness drives him further into himself: in attempting to escape the war he shuts out involvement with his men. As he leaves Sadie's, one of his men stops him and says innocently, "Hello, Captain. You're leaving early, aren't you?" Brandon gruffly snaps back, "I got here early."

Outside the bar, an old Chinese gentleman offers to sell Brandon his daughter. Cliff snaps his lighter, looks at her and she slowly turns her face up to look back at him. Brandon gives the old man some money but says, "No thanks." The girl, Shu-Jen (Li Li Hua), misunderstands Cliff's rejection of her and follows him to his place to become a servant in his house. As in *Seventh Heaven* and *Man's Castle*, the girl's presence in Brandon's quarters transforms them into a home. Her tidying up, cooking and scrubbing seem to originate more in her love for him than in her debt to him. Though he still goes out to get drunk at Sadie's, he now takes off his muddy boots when he returns and looks in on Shu-Jen and Ellington, a war orphan who lives with them as chaperon. After one late-night return from Sadie's, Cliff drunkenly staggers over to Shu-Jen's bed to cover her up with a blanket, then turns to Ellington and salutes the sleeping boy. Shu-Jen and Ellington become a kind of family for Brandon: his growing responsiveness to their concern for him breaks down his insularity against the world; he begins to drink less and to get along better with his crew.

There is a great moment near the end of *Disputed Passage* when Audrey sits at the bedside of Beaven who lies unconscious in a recently bombed Chinese hospital. Borzage pans from Beaven and the girl to a hole in the roof through which we can see stars shining. The night dissolves into the dawn and Borzage pans back down to Audrey and Beaven as the latter miraculously awakens from his coma. The pan here not only integrates the characters into their setting but also associates Beaven's recovery with a divinely regenerative force as mysterious as the dawning of a new day. The relationship between Cliff and Shu-Jen in *China Doll* results in a similar sort of therapeutic restoration to life. One night, Cliff has a sudden attack of malaria and returns home trembling with chills. Shu-Jen, like the heroine of *The River*, crawls into bed with Cliff to warm him with the heat of her body. Outside, a storm begins to rage. As the two lie together, Borzage pans up from Cliff's delirium to a window high above the bed through which we see lightning flashing. Before our eyes, the dark storm slowly dissolves into the bright dawn and the camera pans back down to reveal the fever broken and Cliff healthy again. This shot, like the one in *Disputed Passage,* becomes a prefiguration of Cliff and Shu-Jen's final redemption in that it suggests not only their sexual union—the fruition of which we see at the end of the film—but also Cliff's more immediate return to health. At the same time, the shot, again like the earlier one in *Disputed Passage*, knits Cliff and Shu-Jen into a larger natural order outside themselves that oversees both their physical and spiritual regeneration.

The culmination of the lovers' relationship occurs months later at the end of the film when Cliff returns from a mission to find the base attacked and destroyed by the enemy, Shu-Jen, now his wife, dead in the wreckage and his new-born daughter missing, presumably dead. Relapsing into his earlier, lonely bitterness, Cliff decides to remain behind to avenge himself on the enemy when they return. As his crew reluctantly takes off, Cliff hears his baby crying somewhere among the ruined remains of the base. Just before the enemy planes return, he finds the infant and takes her to safety under the wheels of a demolished vehicle, first fastening his dog tags around her neck. In the midst of a tremendously chaotic action sequence with the camera now in the air with the enemy, now on the ground with Brandon, Borzage cuts back and forth from Brandon, machine-gunning enemy planes, to the baby he is fighting to

CHINA DOLL: Cliff (Victor Mature) discovers the body of his dead wife, Shu-Jen (Li Li Hua) in the wreckage of the air base

protect. As the action grows more frenetic, the pace of the cutting between Cliff and his child quickens, binding the two together and achieving Cliff's rebirth not in his own body but in that of his child.

In *I've Always Loved You* and *Moonrise*, Borzage shows the source of the destructive forces which haunt his central characters: the first concert in which Goronoff becomes Myra's master and the vividly expressionistic execution of Danny's father seem to cause Myra and Danny's melancholic isolation and inability to find happiness. In *China Doll*, Cliff's bitter loneliness and hate have no specific source; therefore, there is no action that will save him. As a result, he becomes a character who is ultimately irredeemable. Brandon

121

can only exorcise the spirits that infect him through his death. Sgt. Foster remarks at one point in the film: "The Greeks say that no one really knows happiness until after he's dead." Though he terribly misquotes "the Greeks," Foster's jumbled philosophy accurately describes the effect of Cliff's death at the end.* He can only find happiness *after* and *through* his death. Though he himself is doomed from the start of the film, Cliff's sacrificial death enables his spirit to triumph, transferred to the body of his child.

The film's epilogue, set years later in an American airport, reveals Cliff's remarkable triumph over time, space, and mortality. Cliff's former crew members greet his teenage daughter on her arrival from China. As she steps out of the plane and walks down the stairs, she identifies herself to her godparents by showing them Cliff's dog tags which she wears around her neck. What makes the girl's radiant appearance at the end so powerful is Borzage's treatment of her not so much as an individual character as the embodiment of Cliff's and Shu-Jen's souls. The girl becomes a living symbol of her parents' regeneration. Like her parents on the night she was conceived, the girl is at one with a larger, divine and eternal order that watches over all human achievement and gives it meaning.

BORZAGE'S VISUAL STYLE

What makes the religious-romantic content of Borzage's films so powerful is the transcendent nature of his visual style. In *Mannequin* (1937), the tangible reality of a flickering light bulb on Jessie's

---

* In Herodotus, Solon tells Croesus that no man can truly be called happy until his life is over, "for oftentimes God gives men a gleam of happiness, and then plunges them into ruin." "Histories," Book I, Ch. 32. The final choral passage and last lines of Sophocles's "Oedipus Tyrannus" read similarly, "Count no mortal happy till he has passed the final limit of his life secure from pain."

(Joan Crawford) tenement stairway is less important than the intangible flickering light it emits. Though the source of the light is shown and Borzage's character can temporarily correct its malfunctioning, the light becomes, like the sound of the train whistle in *Man's Castle,* an intangible force that cannot be dealt with physically: later that night the light flickers again and finally goes out, trapping Jessie in the darkness of the stairway. Though the flickering light is part of a physical environment (Hester Street) that Jessie is trying to escape, Borzage treats it as a visual metaphor for the atmosphere that surrounds her.

In a way, Borzage's visual style reflects his belief in the immateriality of objects and characters. His images have little to do with real things; rather, like Plato's ideal forms, they refer to an absolute and eternal reality that exists on a purely abstract level. In other words, Borzage's images often function as spiritual metaphors, revealing the director's concern for larger issues outside the action itself. In *Strange Cargo,* Cambreau draws a map of an escape route from the island's prison in a Bible and leaves it behind for Verne to use when he escapes and follows Cambreau and the other prisoners. Though Borzage only cuts to the Bible-map twice, the image becomes one of the most powerful in the film, representing the symbolic aspects of the prisoners' journey. The explicitness of this brief image, consistent with the explicitness of the film as a whole, illustrates the depth of Borzage's commitment, on a visual level, to the metaphorical aspects of his story.

In visual terms, Borzage's backgrounds, like his tonal environments, have a spiritual rather than material quality. In most of his films, Borzage uses studio sets and, as a result, his backgrounds have an unreal, fairy-tale quality. His sets and characters often seem to glow with an other-worldly luminescence. Part of this has to do with the way Borzage lights them—the tones of his backgrounds, often as light as or lighter than his characters' faces, give his frames a weightless quality. Borzage's lighting, like Griffith's, is consistent throughout the frame; each part of the frame seems equally and evenly lit. But Borzage's lighting is softer than Griffith's and his frames lack Griffith's precision and tremendous resolution in depth. What is important about Borzage's lighting is that it creates an *evenness* of tone within the frame: though the background and foreground are weightless, they are equally weightless. As a result of this, specific objects or backgrounds never exert, as they do in Hawks, specific physical force on Borzage's characters. The force that the stove in *Man's Castle* and the mirror-dresser in *Little Man, What Now?* exert on the characters is a spiritual force. The relationships of Borzage's characters to objects or to their backgrounds, because of this evenness of tone, do not work out in spatial terms; one cannot speak of conflict between foreground and background or of that between characters and their environment. The flatness of Borzage's backgrounds and their tendency to fall out of focus in medium shot and close-up do not, as they do in Cukor's films, separate characters from their backgrounds by dividing the frame into two planes of depth. Instead, Borzage's lighting unifies his frame into a single level of depth and into a single *tonal* unity of foreground and background. In other words, characters do not derive their spirituality from specific objects in the frame or from specific parts of the frame, as in Griffith, but from the tonal quality of the whole frame and the succession of frames around it, by editing rhythms imposed upon the characters from a logic that exists outside the frame itself.

Unlike that of Hawks, Borzage's visual style is anti-materialistic. At the beginning of *Three Comrades,* after the transcendent toast to the "comrades living and dead of all men," Borzage introduces his central characters. When one of them, Otto Koster, learns that, because of the armistice, his plane is to be dismantled, he leaves the group and goes outside. Outside, Borzage tracks in on Koster as he approaches his plane. He cuts to an insert shot of a medallion with "Baby" written on it, cuts back to the original set-up as Koster takes the pin out of a grenade, drops it into the plane's cockpit and walks away. Then Borzage cuts back to a shot which tracks away from the plane and from Koster. The camera tracks back until the grenade explodes; then it tracks back towards the burning plane.

What makes the scene so emphatic is its simplicity and economy. Though the editing helps make the action dramatic, the force that the scene has hinges on the tracking camera that pulls away from the plane. The tracking shot denies the plane's physical reality, removing us from it as a real object and turning it into an image reflecting that object, just as the track-in later on Pat's x-ray calls attention to its function as something representative of material reality but also something which, in itself, is flat and unreal. In terms of Borzage's visual style, material objects have no material reality: they are only *representative* of material reality. Though Koster destroys his aeroplane, it's clear that whatever "Baby" is will live on after the demise of its physical reality. In fact, we later see an insert shot of the same medallion on Koster's car, an object which he also sacrifices to achieve a larger goal—to pay for Pat's operation. The scene epitomises the whole film: characters give objects and one another, through friendship and love, some sort of life of their own that goes beyond material existence. Both the objects and Borzage's characters attain an "eternal" reality—something impervious to time and space, to death or physical separation.

There is a sequence in *Man's Castle* in which Bill, afraid of becoming trapped by Trina's love, leaves her. The scene begins with a two-shot close-up of them together. Bill slowly draws out of the frame, leaving Trina alone on the bed. A train whistle is heard on the soundtrack. After a few moments, Borzage cuts to Bill hopping a freight. Then he begins to cross-cut, first back to Trina, then to Bill. The shots of Trina have tremendous power, partly because of

MAN'S CASTLE: Trina draws Bill back through space.
Frame enlargement

her angled position in the frame, and suggest a strength more abstract than physical. As if her image were drawing him back through space, Bill first looks back and then jumps off the train to return to her. Borzage's cross-cuts here, somewhat like Griffith's in *Intolerance* or *Way Down East,* go beyond the mere mechanics of suspense. Implying an ultimate rescue, they attain a redemptive force.

In Borzage's films, as suggested above, the space between characters—even those in a single frame—has no deterministic reality.

Where Welles, in the famous stairway sequences in *The Magnificent Ambersons*, shows the separation of his characters in geographically physical terms—in fact, the space between characters becomes a character itself—Borzage has an altogether non-physical conception of time and space. The split-screen phone conversations in *Three Comrades* convey this: one character in one spatial matrix can communicate with another in another spatial matrix. The use of the splitscreen foreshadows a sort of relationship, like that in *Man's Castle* or *I've Always Loved You*, that can overcome space. The physical separation of the lovers throughout *Three Comrades* develops the spirituality of their relationship. Like Koster's plane, it can be seen as another physical reality that Borzage's visual style destroys and transcends. As a result, the form dissolve from Pat and the Christmas tree in the mountain sanitarium to Erich and the Christmas tree in Alphons's café, like that from Mrs. Dexter's radio to the arched interior of Dean Harcourt's church in *Green Light*, transcends the physical reality of space by suggesting a far greater, spiritual reality that overshadows and encompasses every action in Borzage's universe.

The shooting of *Three Comrades*, like that of Borzage's other Thirties work, has a strange, possessed quality to it, as if Borzage were trying to capture in his images the intangible forces that surround his characters. One sequence in particular, the time montage that announces the changing of the seasons, illustrates the completeness of Borzage's "romanticised" view of the universe. Midway through the film, Borzage cuts to shots of the wind blowing through the trees and through city streets when winter comes. He transforms an intangible thing like time into an almost mystical force that floats his cork-like characters along, much as the unseen wind does the newspaper in the streets.

At the end of *Three Comrades*, almost every shot seems to capture the spiritual essence of Borzage's characters. The breathtakingly beautiful crane shot as Pat gets out of bed after her operation and goes to her balcony to see Erich and Koster for the last time suggests, as does the overhead shooting at the end of *Seventh Heaven* and *Till We Meet Again*, a supernatural presence that dictates Pat's ultimate transcendence of the final physical barrier which separates her from Erich: her body.

Borzage ends the film in a cemetery outside the city and shows the three comrades and Pat reunited—a realisation of the film's first lines that toasted "the comrades living and dead of all men." In the last shot, Erich and Koster, surrounded by the ethereal images of Pat and Gottfried, leave the cemetery and talk of going to South America. Like the characters at the end of *Man's Castle* escaping on the train together or those of *Little Man, What Now?* with the prospect of a better life in Holland, Borzage's characters here do not run away from their chaotic, troubled backgrounds as much as they grow out of them spiritually. Borzage so totally transforms them that it becomes impossible for his surviving characters to return to their former lives. Erich and Koster, like the dead Pat and Gottfried, find liberation from the weight of their own bodies and chaotic backgrounds.

What makes Borzage's melodramas unique is his avoidance of extreme conflicts: his characters and their environment are not in mortal conflict. Rather than externalising his plots into moral contests between good and evil in which characters defeat or are defeated by the evil that threatens to engulf them, Borzage, diffusing the conventional melodramatic moral polarity, permits the co-existence of several moral and spiritual systems in his films. He merely makes a trial of one by contrasting it with another, providing the catalyst for his characters' growth out of one order and emergence into another, transcendent one. For Borzage, it is only through love and adversity that souls are made great.

FRANK BORZAGE Filmography*

Frank Borzage (bor-zay-dzhee) was born on April 23, 1893, in Salt Lake City, Utah. He died on June 19, 1962. At the age of thirteen he worked in a silver mine to pay for a correspondence school course in acting. In 1906, he joined an acting company that toured the country as a prop boy and, three years later, became an actor himself (once playing five parts in a single production of "Hamlet"). In 1913, after drifting around the country as an actor and living in boxcars and tents, Borzage arrived in Hollywood where he became a part of Thomas Ince's production company, playing bit parts as a $5-a-day extra. After several years of playing stock villains in Ince westerns and playing in some Mutual comedies, Borzage began to direct his own films. He won Academy Awards for his direction of *Seventh Heaven* (1927) and *Bad Girl* (1931). A few months before his death in 1962 he received the D. W. Griffith Award "for outstanding contributions in the field of film directing" from the Directors Guild of America. Two of Borzage's brothers, Lew and Danny, also worked in the motion picture industry. Lew produced a number of his brother's most successful films and Danny became a member of director John Ford's production staff.

As an actor, Frank Borzage appeared in the following films:** Undated:

NIGHT OF THE TRAIL, TWO BITS, UNLUCKY LUKE, MATCHIN' JIM.

1912. WHEN LEE SURRENDERS, ON SECRET SERVICE, THE BLOOD WILL TELL.

1913. THE AMBASSADOR'S ENVOY, THE DRUMMER OF THE EIGHTH, THE PRIDE OF THE SOUTH, DAYS OF '49, THE CRIMSON STAIN, THE WAR CORRESPONDENT, A DIXIE MOTHER, THE LOADED DICE, YOUTH, JEALOUSY, BRIDE OF LONESOME, A FOREIGN SPY, THE MYSTERY OF THE YELLOW ASTER MINE, A CRAKS MAN SANTA CLAUS, RETRIBUTION, A HOPE LEGEND.

1914. THE WHEEL OF LIFE, A FLASH IN THE DARK, LOVE'S WESTERN FLIGHT, THE BATTLE OF GETTYSBURG, THE WRATH OF THE GODS, THE TYPHOON, A NEW ENGLAND IDYL, THE SILENT MESSENGER, THE ROMANCE OF THE SAWDUST RING, DESERT GOLD, THE CUP OF LIFE.

1915. THE DESPERADO, IN THE SAGE BRUSH COUNTRY (MR. NOBODY), A RELIC OF OLD JAPAN, A CROOK'S SWEETHEART, PARSON LARKIN'S WIFE, A CHILD OF THE

° Material in this filmography is based on information contained in Henri Agel's monograph on Borzage (Anthologie du Cinéma), Jean Mitry's "Universal Filmography" and the American Film Institute's "Catalogue of Feature Films" (1921–1930). Additional material was provided by Anthony Slide.

** This list of Borzage's screen appearances is most likely incomplete.

TURF, MOLLY OF THE MOUNTAINS, THE AWAKENING, THE DISILLUSIONMENT OF JANE, THE SPARK FROM THE EMBERS, HER ALIBI, TOOLS OF PROVIDENCE, THE HAMMER, A FRIEND IN NEED, ALIAS JAMES CHAUFFEUR, TOURING WITH TILLIE, HER ADOPTED FATHER, ALMOST A WIDOW, ANITA'S BUTTERFLY, MAKING OVER FATHER, NOBODY'S HOME, TWO HEARTS AND A THIEF.

1916. JACK, THE PILGRIM, ONE TO THE MINUTE.

Frank Borzage directed the following films.

Silent Films

THAT GAL OF BURKE'S (1916). *With:* Anna Little, Frank Borzage.

MAMMY'S ROSE (1916). *Co-dir:* James Douglass. *Sc:* James Douglass. *With:* Frank Borzage, Neva Gerber, Antrim Short. Released by American Mutual.

LIFE'S HARMONY (1916). *Co-dir:* Lorimer Johnston. *Sc:* Lorimer Johnston. *With:* Vivian Rich, Alfred Vosburgh, Frank Borzage, Antrim Short. Released by American Mutual.

THE SILKEN SPIDER (1916). *With:* Vivian Rich, Frank Borzage.

THE CODE OF HONOR (1916). *With:* Estella Allan, Frank Borzage.

NELL DALE'S MEN FOLKS (1916). *With:* Anna Little, Frank Borzage. Released by American Mutual.

THE FORGOTTEN PRAYER (1916). *With:* Anna Little, Frank Borzage.

THE COURTIN' OF CALLIOPE CLEW (1916). *With:* Anna Little, Frank Borzage.

NUGGET JIM'S PARDNER (1916). Comedy. *With:* Anna Little, Frank Borzage, Jack Farrell, Dick La Reno. Released by American Mutual on two reels.

THE DEMON OF FEAR (1916). *With:* Anna Little, Frank Borzage. Released by American Mutual on two reels.

LAND O' LIZARDS (1916). *With:* Frank Borzage. Released by American Mutual. 4,600 ft. Reissued in 1922 as SILENT SHELBY.

IMMEDIATE LEE (1916). Western. Cowboy battles the rustlers who cost him his job and scarred his face; he wins the love of a dance-hall girl. *With:* Frank Borzage (*Immediate Lee*), Anna Little (*Beulah*), Chick Morrison (*John Masters*), Jack Richardson (*Kentucky Hurley*). Released by American Mutual. 4,600 ft. Reissued in 1922 as HAIR TRIGGER CASEY.

ENCHANTMENT (1916). *Sc:* Frank Borzage. *With:* Vivian Rich, Alfred Vosburgh, Frank Borzage, Antrim Short. Released by American Mutual.

THE PRIDE AND THE MAN (1916). *Sc:* Frank Borzage. *With:* William Russell, Gertrude Short, Antrim Short, Frank Borzage. Released by American Mutual.

DOLLARS OF DROSS (1916). *Sc:* Frank Borzage. *With:* Vivian Rich, Alfred Vosburgh, Louise Lester, George Periolat. Released by American Mutual.

WEE LADY BETTY (1917). *Co-dir:* Charles Miller. *Sc:* Catherine Carr. *Ph:* Pliny Horne. *With:* Bessie Love, Frank Borzage, Charles K. French, Walt Whitman, Aggie Herring. *Prod:* Allan Dwan for Triangle Corp.

FLYING COLORS (1917). *Sc:* Monte S. Katterjohn. *Ph:* Pliny Horne. *With:* William Desmond, Alma Rubens, J. Barney Sherry, Joseph King. Released by Triangle Corp.

UNTIL THEY GET ME (1917). A Canadian Mountie spends seven years tracking down a killer. Sc: Monte S. Katterjohn. Ph: C. H. Wales. With: Jack Curtis (Kirby), Joe King (Richard Selwyn), Wilbur Higbee (Superintendent Draper), Pauline Starke (Margy), Walter Perry (Sgt. Blaney). Prod: Allan Dwan for Triangle Corp.

THE ATOM (1918). Sc: Catherine Carr. Ph: Pliny Horne. With: Pauline Starke (Jenny), Harry Mestayer (Montague Booth), Belle Bennett (Belle Hathaway), Tom Buckingham, Frank Borzage. Prod: Allan Dwan for Triangle Corp.

THE GUN WOMAN (1918). Sc: Monte S. Katterjohn. Ph: Pliny Horne. With: Texas Guinan, Darrell Foss, Francis McDonald, Frank Borzage. Prod: Allan Dwan for Triangle Corp.

SHOES THAT DANCED (1918). Story of a New York gang war between the Hudson Dusters and the Cherry Hills. Sc: Jack Cunningham (story by John A. Morosco). Ph: Pliny Horne. With: Pauline Starke (Rhoda Regan), Anna Dodge (Mrs. Regan), Lydia Yeamans Titus (Mother Carey), Wallace MacDonald (Harmony Lad), Dick Rosson (Stumpy). Prod: Allan Dwan for Triangle Corp.

INNOCENT'S PROGRESS (1918). Candy store girl, lured by false promises of a married man, goes to the city, discovers his deception and meets a rich man who first adopts, then marries her. Sc: Catherine Carr (story by Frances Quinlan). Ph: Pliny Horne. With: Pauline Starke (Tessa Fayne), Lillian West (Madeline Carson), Alice Knowland (Aunt Lottie), Jack Livingston (Carey

Larned), Charles Dorian (Olin Humphreys), Graham Pett (Masters). Prod: Allan Dwan for Triangle Corp.

AN HONEST MAN (1918). Sc: Monte S. Katterjohn. Ph: Pliny Horne. With: William Desmond (Benny Boggs), Mary Warren (Beatrice Burnett), Claire Anderson, William Franey, Charles K. French. Prod: Allan Dwan for Triangle Corp.

SOCIETY FOR SALE (1918). Sc: Monte S. Katterjohn. Ph: Pliny Horne. With: William Desmond (Honorable Billy), Gloria Swanson (Phyllis Clyne), Herbert Prior (Lord Sheldon), Lillian Langdon (Lady Mary), Charles Dorian, Lillian West, Claire Anderson. Prod: Allan Dwan for Triangle.

WHO IS TO BLAME? (1918). Sc: Monte Katterjohn (story by E. Magnus Ingleton). Ph: Pliny Horne. With: Jack Abbe (Taru), Jack Livingston (Grant Barton), Lillian West (Tonia Marsh), Maud Wayne (Marion Craig), Lillian Langdon (Mrs. Craig). Released by Triangle Corp.

THE GHOST FLOWER (1918). Poor Neapolitan girl, promised in marriage to a murderer, runs off with a violinist who is killed by her fiancé. Sc: Monte Katterjohn and Catherine Carr. With: Alma Rubens (Giulia), Charles West (La-Farge), Francis MacDonald (Tony Cafarelli), Dick Rosson (Paola), Emory Hohnson (Duke de Chaumont), Naida Lessing (Laserena), Tote Ducrow (Ercolano).

THE CURSE OF IKU (1918). A Japanese house servant kidnaps a guest's fiancée, takes her to Japan and is pursued by her lover. Sc: Catherine Carr. With: Frank Borzage (Allen Carrol III), Tsuru

Aoki (*Omi San*). Released by Essanay. 7 reels.

TOTON (1919). *Sc:* Catherine Carr. *Ph:* Jack MacKenzie. *With:* Olive Thomas (*Toton*), Norman Kerry (*Lane*), Francis McDonald (*Pierre*), Jack Perrin (*Carew*). Released by Triangle Corp. 6 reels.

PRUDENCE OF BROADWAY (1919). *Sc:* Catherine Carr. *Ph:* Pliny Horne. *With:* Olive Thomas.

WHOM THE GODS DESTROY (1919). *Sc:* Catherine Carr (story by Cyrus Townsend Brady). *With:* Pauline Starke, Kathryn Adams, Jack Mulhall. Released by First National.

ASHES OF DESIRE (1919). *Sc:* Sam Small, Jr. *With:* Alma Rubens, Walter McGrail. Released by Essanay. 6 reels.

HUMORESQUE (1920). Melodrama. A story of mother love. *Sc:* Frances Marion (story by Fannie Hurst). *Ph:* Gilbert Warrenton. *With:* Alma Rubens (*Gina Berg*), Vera Gordon (*Mama Kantor*), Dore Davidson (*Abraham Kantor*), Gaston Glass (*Leon Kantor, man*), Bobby Connelly (*Leon Kantor, boy*), Sidney Carlyle (*Mannie Kantor*), Helen Connelly, Ann Wallick, Joseph Cooper, Maurice Levigne, Alfred Goldberg, Edward Stanton, Miriam Battista. A Cosmopolitan Production. Released by Paramount Pictures. 6 reels.

THE DUKE OF CHIMNEY BUTTE (1921). Western. Peddler becomes a cowboy and helps girl rancher combat cattle rustlers. *Sc:* Marian Ainslee (story by George Washington Ogden). *Ph:* Jack MacKenzie. *With:* Fred Stone (*Jeremeah Lambert*), Vola Vale (*Vesta Philbrook*), Josie Sedgwick (*Grace Kerr*), Chick Morrison (*Kerr, the son*), Buck Connors (*Taters*), Harry Dunkinson (*Jedlick*). *Prod:* Andrew J. Callaghan for Fred Stone Productions. 4,600 ft.

GET-RICH-QUICK WALLINGFORD (1921). Comedy. Two con artists persuade small town to invest in a phony covered-carpet-tack scheme and are forced to turn honest. *Sc:* Luther Reed (play by George M. Cohan based on George Randolph Chester's Wallingford stories). *Ph:* Chester Lyons. *Art dir:* Joseph Urban. *With:* Sam Hardy (*J. Rufus Wallingford*), Norman Kerry ("*Blackie*" *Daw*), Doris Kenyon (*Fannie Jasper*), Diana Allen (*Gertrude Dempsey*), Edgar Nelson (*Eddie Lamb*), Billie Dove (*Dorothy Wells*), Mrs. Charles Willard (*Mrs. Dempsey*), Eugene Keith (*Harkins*), William Carr, William Robyns, Theodore Westman, Jr., Patterson Dial, Jerry Sinclair, Benny One. Released by Paramount Pictures. 7,381 ft.

BACK PAY (1922). Melodrama. Country girl rejects home town boy friend for an exciting life in the city but marries him when he returns home wounded from the war. *Sc:* Frances Marion (story by Fannie Hurst). *Ph:* Chester Lyons. *Art dir:* Joseph Urban. *With:* Seena Owen (*Hester Bevins*), Matt Moore (*Jerry Newcombe*), J. Barney Sherry (*Charles G. Wheeler*), Ethel Duray (*Kitty*), Charles Craig ("*Speed*"), Jerry Sinclair (*Thomas Craig*). A Cosmopolitan Production. Released by Paramount Pictures. 6,460 ft.

BILLY JIM (1922). Western. Wealthy cattleman pretends he is a cowboy and protects a girl's property from claim jumpers. *Sc:* Frank Howard Clark (story by Jackson Gregory). *With:* Fred Stone (*Billy Jim*), Millicent Fisher (*Martha Dunforth*), George Hernandez (*Dudley

Dunforth), William Bletcher (*Jimmy*), Marian Skinner (*Mrs. Dunforth*), Frank Thorne (*Roy Forsythe*). *Prod:* Andrew J. Callaghan for Fred Stone Productions. 4,900 ft.

THE GOOD PROVIDER (1922). Melodrama. After years of prosperity, the business of a Jewish immigrant fails; he tries to take his own life but finds new hope in a partnership with his daughter's fiancé. *Sc:* John Lynch (story by Fannie Hurst). *Ph:* Chester Lyons. *With:* Vera Gordon (*Becky Binswanger*), Dore Davidson (*Julius Binswanger*), Miriam Battista (*Pearl Binswanger*), Vivienne Osborne (*Pearl Binswanger*), William Collier, Jr. (*Izzy Binswanger*), John Roche (*Max Teitlebaum*), Ora Jones (*Mrs. Teitlebaum*), Edward Philips, Muriel Martin, James Devine, Blanche Craig, Margaret Severn. A Cosmopolitan Production. Paramount Pictures. 7,753 ft.

VALLEY OF SILENT MEN (1922). Canadian western. A seriously wounded man confesses to murders committed by a friend but is redeemed when his friend admits his crimes. *Sc:* John Lynch (story by James Oliver Curwood). *Ph:* Chester Lyons. *With:* Alma Rubens (*Marette Radison*), Lew Cody (*Cpl. James Kent*), Joseph King ("*Buck" O'Connor*), Mario Majeroni (*Pierre Radison*), George Nash (*Inspector Kedsty*), J. W. Johnston (*Jacques Radison*). A Cosmopolitan Production. Released by Paramount Pictures. 6,500 ft.

THE PRIDE OF PALOMAR (1922). Melodrama. Son returns from the war to find his father dead and his ranch stolen. *Sc:* Grant Carpenter and John Lynch (story by Peter Bernard Kyne).

Ph: Chester Lyons. *With:* Forrest Stanley (*Don Mike Farrell*), Marjorie Daw (*Kay Parker*), Tote Du Crow (*Pablo*), James Barrows (*Father Dominic*), Joseph Dowling (*Don Miguel*), Alfred Allen (*John Parker*), George Nichols (*Conway*), Warner Oland (*Okada*), Mrs. Jessie Hebbard, Percy Williams, Mrs. George Hernandez, Edward Brady, Carmen Arselle. A Cosmopolitan Production. Released by Paramount Pictures. 7,494 ft.

THE NTH COMMANDMENT (1923). Shopgirl leaves boyfriend for another but returns and marries him when she learns he has consumption. *Sc:* Frances Marion (story by Fannie Hurst). *Ph:* Chester Lyons. *With:* Coleen Moore (*Sarah Juke*), James Morrison (*Harry Smith*), Eddie Philips (*Jimmie Fitzgibbons*), Charlotte Merriam (*Angine Sprunt*), George Cooper (*Max Plute*). *Prod:* Frances Marion for Cosmopolitan Productions. Released by Paramount Pictures. 7,339 ft.

CHILDREN OF DUST (1923). Melodrama. Orphan saves the life of his rival during the war and later wins the girl. *Sc:* Agnes Christine Johnston and Frank Dazey (story by Tristram Tupper). *Ph:* Chester Lyons. *Art dir:* Frank Ormston. *Ed:* H. P. Bretherton. *With:* Bert Woodruff (*Old Archer*), Johnnie Walker (*Terwilliger, the man*), Frankie Lee (*Terwilliger, the boy*), Pauline Garon (*Helen Raymond, the woman*), Josephine (*Helen Raymond, the girl*), Lloyd Hughes (*Harvey Livermore, the man*), Newton Hall (*Harvey Livermore, the boy*), George Nichols (*Terwilliger's stepfather*). *Prod:* Arthur H. Jacobs for First National Pictures. 6,228 ft.

AGE OF DESIRE (1923). Boy poses as the lost son of a rich woman and discovers that he actually is her son. *Sc:* Mary O'Hara, Lenore Coffee and Dixie Wilson. *Ph:* Chester Lyons. *Art dir:* Frank Ormston. *With:* Joseph Swickard (*Marcio*), William Collier, Jr. (*Ranny at 21*), Frank Truesdell (*Malcolm Trask*), Bruce Guerin (*Ranny at 3*), Frankie Lee (*Ranny at 13*), J. Farrell MacDonald (*Dan Reagan*), Mary Jane Irving (*Margy at 10*), Myrtle Stedman (*Janet Loring*), Aggie Herring (*Ann Reagan*), Mary Philbin (*Margy at 18*), Edithe Yorke (*Gran'ma*). *Prod:* Arthur H. Jacobs for First National Pictures. 5,174 ft.

SECRETS (1924). Wife, tending her sick husband, sleeps, dreams of their past together and awakens to find him cured. *Sc:* Frances Marion (play by Rudolph Besier and May Edginton). *Ph:* Tony Gaudio. *With:* Norma Talmadge (*Mary Marlowe Carlton*), Eugene O'-Brien (*John Carlton*), Patterson Dial (*Susan*), Emily Fitzroy (*Mrs. Marlowe*), Claire McDowell (*Elizabeth Channing*), George Nichols (*William Marlowe*), Harvey Clark (*Bob*), Charles Ogle (*Dr. McGovern*), Francis Feeny (*John Carlton Jr.*), Alice Day, Winston Miller, May Giraci, Gertrude Astor, Winter Hall, Frank Elliot, George Cowl, Clarissa Selwynne, Florence Wix. *Prod:* Joseph M. Schenck for First National. 8,363 ft.

THE LADY (1925). Melodrama. Widow, separated from her son by her father-in-law, meets the boy when he is fully grown. *Sc:* Frances Marion (story by Martin Brown). *Ph:* Tony Gaudio. *With:* Norma Talmadge (*Polly Pearl*), Wallace MacDonald (*Leonard St. Au-*

byns), Brandon Hurst (*St. Aubyns, Sr.*), Alf Goulding (*Tom Robinson*), Doris Lloyd (*Fannie St. Clair*), Walter Long (*Blackie*), George Hackathorne (*Leonard Cairns*), Marc MacDermott (*Mr. Wendover*), Emily Fitzroy (*Madame Blanche*), Paulette Duval, John Fox, Jr., John Herdman, Margaret Seddon, Edwin Hubbell, Miles McCarthy. *Prod:* Joseph M. Schenck for Norma Talmadge Productions. Released by First National Pictures. 7,357 ft.

DADDY'S GONE A-HUNTING (1925). A wife's earnings send her artist-husband to Paris to study; after his return, they separate. *Sc:* Kenneth B. Clarke (from novel by Zoe Atkins). *Ph:* Chester Lyons. *Art dir:* Cedric Gibbons. *Ed:* Frank Sullivan. *With:* Alice Joyce (*Edith*), Percy Marmont (*Julian*), Virginia Marshall (*Janet*), Helena D'Algy (*Olga*), Ford Sterling (*Oscar*), Holmes Herbert (*Greenough*), Edythe Chapman (*Mrs. Greenough*), James Barrows, James Macellhern, Charles Crockett, Kate Toncray. *Prod:* Louis B. Mayer for Metro-Goldwyn Pictures. 5,851 ft.

WAGES FOR WIVES (1925). Comedy. Wife goes on strike when her husband ignores her marriage agreement to split his pay-check fifty-fifty with her. *Sc:* Kenneth B. Clarke (play by Guy Bolton and Winchell Smith). *Ph:* Ernest G. Palmer. *With:* Jacqueline Logan (*Nell Bailey*), Creighton Hale (*Danny Kester*), Earle Foxe (*Hughie Logan*), ZaSu Pitts (*Luella Logan*), Claude Gillingwater (*Jim Bailey*), David Butler (*Chester Logan*), Margaret Seddon (*Annie Bailey*), Margaret Livingston, Dan Mason, Tom Ricketts. *Prod:* William Fox for Fox Film Corp. 6,650 ft.

LAZYBONES (1925). Comedy-melodrama. Rural town's laziest citizen rescues girl from drowning and adopts her child—with whom, years later, he falls in love. *Sc:* Frances Marion (story by Owen Davis). *Ph:* Glen MacWilliams and George Schneiderman. *With:* Buck Jones (*Lazybones*), Madge Bellamy (*Kit*), Virginia Marshall (*Kit, as a child*), Edythe Chapman (*Mrs. Tuttle*), Leslie Fenton (*Dick Ritchie*), Jane Novak (*Agnes Fanning*), Emily Fitzroy (*Mrs. Fanning*), ZaSu Pitts (*Ruth Fanning*), William Norton Bailey (*Elmer Ballister*). *Prod:* William Fox for Fox Film Corp. 7,234 ft.

THE CIRCLE 1925). Comedy-drama. Wife, using the earlier elopement of her parents-in-law as a model for herself, plans to run away with another man. *Sc:* Kenneth B. Clarke (play by W. Somerset Maugham). *Ph:* Chester Lyons. *Art dir:* Cedric Gibbons and James Basevi. *With:* Eleanor Boardman (*Elizabeth*), Malcolm McGregor (*Edward Lutton*), Alec Francis (*Lord Clive Cheney*), Eugenie Besserer (*Lady Catherine*), George Fawcett (*Portenous*), Creighton Hale (*Arnold*), Otto Hoffman (*Dorker*), Eulalie Jensen (*Mrs. Shenstone*). Released by M-G-M Pictures. 5,511 ft.

THE FIRST YEAR (1926). Comedy. Newlyweds invite husband's important business acquaintance to a disastrous dinner. *Sc:* Frances Marion (play by Frank Craven). *Ph:* Chester Lyons. *With:* Matt Moore (*Tom Tucher*), Kathryn Perry (*Grace Livingston*), John Patrick (*Dick Loring*), Frank Currier (*Dr. Livingston*), Frank Cooley (*Mr. Livingston*), Virginia Madison (*Mrs. Livingston*), Carolynne Snowden (*Hattie*), J. Farrell

MacDonald (*Mr. Barstow*). *Prod:* William Fox for Fox Film Corp. 6,038 ft.

THE DIXIE MERCHANT (1926). Comedy-drama. After an automobile accident, a family splits up only to be reunited when their horse wins a race. *Sc:* Kenneth B. Clarke (story by John Barry Benefield). *Ph:* Frank B. Good. *With:* J. Farrell MacDonald (*Jean Paul Fippany*), Madge Bellamy (*Aida Fippany*), Jack Mulhall (*Jimmy Pickett*), Claire MacDowell (*Josephine Fippany*), Harvey Clark (*Baptiste*), Edward Martindel (*John Pickett*), Evelyn Arden, Onest Conley, Paul Panzer. *Prod:* William Fox for Fox Film Corp. 5,126 ft.

EARLY TO WED (1926). Comedy-drama. Young couple, living beyond their means on the installment plan, lose everything but win the friendship of a millionaire. *Sc:* Kenneth B. Clarke (story by Evelyn Campbell). *Ph:* Ernest G. Palmer. *With:* Matt Moore (*Tommy Carter*), Kathryn Perry (*Daphne Carter*), Albert Gran (*Cassius Hayden*), Julia Swayne Gordon (*Mrs. Hayden*), Arthur Housman (*Art Nevers*), Rodney Hildebrand (*Mike Dugan*), ZaSu Pitts (*Mrs Dugan*), Belva McKay (*Mrs. Nevers*), Ross McCutcheon (*Bill Dugan*), Harry Bailey (*Pelton Jones*). *Prod:* William Fox for Fox Film Corp. 5,912 ft.

"MARRIAGE LICENSE?" (1926). Melodrama. Noble English family rejects son's Canadian wife and engineer their divorce; years later, husband acknowledges his son by re-marrying his wife. *Sc:* Bradley King (play by F. Tennyson Jesse and Harold Marsh Harwood). *Ph:* Ernest Palmer. *With:* Alma Rubens (*Wanda Heriot*), Walter McGrail (*Marcus Heriot*), Richard Walling (*Robin*),

THE RIVER: Allen John (Charles Farrell) escapes the whirlpool and restores Rosalie's soul. Frame enlargement

THE RIVER: Rosalie (Mary Duncan) and Marsdon's crow. Frame enlargement

Walter Pidgeon (*Paul*), Charles Lane (*Sir John*), Emily Fitzroy (*Lady Heriot*), Langhorne Burton (*Cheriton*), Edgar Norton (*Beadon*), George Cowl (*Abercrombie*). *Prod:* William Fox for Fox Film Corp. 7,168 ft.

SEVENTH HEAVEN (1927). Melodrama. Parisian sewer worker takes in a destitute girl, falls in love with her but, before their marriage, is separated from her by the war. *Sc:* Benjamin Glazer, Katherine Hilliker and H. H. Caldwell (story by Austin Strong). *Ph:* Ernest Palmer. *Art dir:* Harry Oliver. *Ed:* Katherine Hilliker and H. H. Caldwell. *With:* Janet Gaynor (*Diane*), Charles Farrell (*Chico*), Ben Bard (*Col. Brissac*), David Butler (*Gobin*), Marie Mosquini (*Madame Gobin*), Albert Gran (*Boul*),

Gladys Brockwell, Emile Chautard, George Stone, Jessie Haslett, Brandon Hurst, Lillian West. *Prod:* William Fox for Fox Film Corp. 8,500 ft. (originally on twelve reels, reduced to nine). Janet Gaynor won an Academy Award for best actress and Frank Borzage won one for best director at the first Academy Awards ceremony.

STREET ANGEL (1928). Melodrama. Young girl, wanted by the police, falls in love with an itinerant artist, is arrested and separated from him on the eve of their marriage. *Sc:* Marion Orth, Katherine Hilliker, H. H. Caldwell, Philip Klein and Henry Roberts Symonds (play by Monckton Hoffe). *Ph:* Ernest Palmer and Paul Ivano. *Ed:* Barney Wolf. *With:* Janet Gaynor (*Angela*), Charles Farrell

(*Gino*), Alberto Rabagliati, Gino Conti (*Policemen*), Guido Trento (*Neri, police sergeant*), Henry Armetta (*Masetto*), Louis Liggett (*Beppo*), Natalie Kingston (*Lisetta*), Milton Dickinson, Helena Herman, David Kashner, Jennie Bruno. *Prod:* William Fox for Fox Film Corp. 9,221 ft. Released both silent and with sound (talking sequences, musical score and sound effects).

THE RIVER (1928). Melodrama. Young man meets girl who has sworn faithfulness to a man now in jail, wins her love and confronts her former lover on his release. *Sc:* Philip Klein, Dwight Cummins and John Hunter Booth (story by Tristram Tupper). *Ph:* Ernest Palmer. *Art dir:* Harry Oliver. *Ed:* Barney Wolf. *Mus:* Maurice Baron and Erno Rapee. Released both silent and with sound (talking sequences and musical score). *With:* Charles Farrell (*Allen John Spender*), Mary Duncan (*Rosalee*), Ivan Linow (*Sam Thompson*), Margaret Mann (*Widow Thompson*), Alfred Sabato (*Marsdon*), Bert Woodruff (*the miller*). *Prod:* William Fox for Fox Film Corp. Silent: 7,704 ft. Sound: 6,536 ft.

LUCKY STAR (1929). Melodrama. Poor farm girl loves one war veteran but her mother plans to marry her to another. *Sc:* Sonya Levien, John Hunter Booth, Katherine Hilliker and H. H. Caldwell (story by Tristram Tupper). *Ph:* Chester Lyons and William Cooper Smith. *Art dir:* Harry Oliver. *Ed:* Katherine Hilliker and H. H. Caldwell. Released both silent and with sound (talking sequences, musical score and sound effects). *With:* Charles Farrell (*Timothy Osborn*), Janet Gaynor (*Mary Tucker*), Big Boy Williams (*Martin Wrenn*), Paul Fix (*Joe*), Hedwig Reicher (*Mrs. Tucker*), Gloria Grey, Hector V. Sarno. *Prod:* William Fox for Fox Film Corp. 8,784 ft.

Sound Films

THEY HAD TO SEE PARIS (1929). Comedy. Oklahoma garage owner discovers oil, fulfils his wife's wishes by taking the family to Paris to expose them to its culture. *Sc:* Sonya Levien, Owen Davis and Wilbur Morse Jr. (story by Homer Croy). *Ph:* Chester Lyons and Al Brick. *Art dir:* Harry Oliver. *Ed:* Margaret V. Clancey. *With:* Will Rogers (*Pike Peters*), Irene Rich (*Mrs. Peters*), Owen Davis, Jr. (*Ross Peters*), Marguerite Churchill (*Opal Peters*), Fifi Dorsay (*Claudine*), Rex Bell (*Clark McCurdy*), Ivan Ledbedeff (*Marquis de Brissac*), Edgar Kennedy (*Ed Eggers*), Bob Kerr, Christine Yves, Marcelle Corday, Theodore Lodi, Marcia Manon, Andre Cheron, Gregory Gaye. *Prod:* William Fox for Fox Film Corp. 96m.

SONG O' MY HEART (1930). Musical melodrama. Irish singer tours America and helps a young couple at home find the happiness he lost. *Sc:* Sonya Levien and Tom Barry (story by Tom Barry and J. J. McCarthy). *Ph:* Chester Lyons, Al Brick and J. O. Taylor. *Art dir:* Harry Oliver. *Ed:* Margaret V. Clancey. *Mus:* Charles Glover, William Kernell, James Hanley, Albert Malotte, C. Mordaunt Spencer. *With:* John McCormack (*Sean O'Carolan*), Alice Joyce (*Mary O'Brien*), Maureen O'Sullivan (*Eileen O'Brien*), Tom Clifford (*Tad O'Brien*), J. M. Kerrigan (*Peter Conlon*), John Gerrick (*Fergus O'Donnel*), Edwin Schneider, J. Farrell MacDonald, Effie Ellsler, Emily Fitzroy, Andres De Segurola, Edward

Martindel. *Prod:* William Fox for Fox Film Corp. 85m.

LILIOM (1930). Allegorical melodrama. To provide for his wife, a man tries to rob a bank, kills himself to avoid capture; but, on his way to heaven, reforms and gets another chance at life. *Sc:* S. N. Behrman and Sonya Levien (play by Ferenc Molnar). *Ph:* Chester Lyons. *Art dir:* Harry Oliver. *Ed:* Margaret V. Clancey. *Mus:* Richard Fall and Marcella Gardner. *With:* Charles Farrell (*Liliom*), Rose Hobart (*Julie*), Estelle Taylor (*Madame Muskat*), Lee Tracy (*Buzzard*), James Marcus (*Linzman*), Walter Abel (*Carpenter*), Mildred Van Dorn (*Marie*), Guinn Williams (*Hollinger*), Lilian Elliot, Bert Roach, H. B. Warner, Dawn O'Day. *Prod:* William Fox for Fox Film Corp. 90m.

AS YOUNG AS YOU FEEL (1931). Comedy. Businessman forces responsibility upon his irresponsible sons by going on a youthful spree with a young French girl. *Sc:* Edwin Burke (play by George Ade). *Ph:* Chester Lyons. *Art dir:* Jack Schulze. *Ed:* Margaret Clancey. *With:* Will Rogers (*Lemeul Morehouse*), Fifi Dorsay (*Fleurette*), Lucien Littlefield (*Mr. Marley*), Donald Dillaway (*Billy Morehouse*), Terrance Ray (*Tom Morehouse*), Lucille Brown (*Dorothy Gregson*), Rosalie Roy (*Rose Gregson*), C. Henry Gordon (*Lamson*), John T. Murray, Brandon Hurst, Marcia Harris, Gregory Gaye. Released by Fox Film Corp. 75m.

DOCTOR'S WIVES (1931). Melodrama. A doctor's wife never gets to see her husband and, as a result, becomes jealously suspicious of one of his female patients. *Sc:* Maurine Watkins and Henry and Sylvia Lieferant. *Ph:* Arthur Edeson. *Ed:* Jack Dennis. *With:* Warner Baxter (*Dr. Judson Penning*), Joan Bennett (*Nina Wyndram*), Victor Varconi (*Dr. Kane Ruyter*), Helene Millard (*Vivian Crosby*), Paul Porcasi (*Dr. Calucci*), Nancy Gardner (*Julia Wyndram*), John St. Polis (*Dr. Mark Wyndram*), Cecilia Loftus (*Aunt Amelia*), George Chandler, Violet Dunn, Ruth Warren, Luise Mackintosh, William Maddox. Released by Fox Film Corp. 80m.

BAD GIRL (1931). Melodrama. Lovers, forced to marry after spending the night together, are beset by financial problems; to pay for his wife's hospital bills the husband agrees to fight a professional boxer. *Sc:* Edwin Burke (from novel by Vina Delmar and play by Vina Delmar and Brian Marlowe). *Ph:* Chester Lyons. *Ed:* Margaret Clancey. *With:* James Dunn (*Edward Collins*), Sally Eilers (*Dorothy Haley*), Minna Gombell (*Edna Driggs*), Frank Darien (*Lathrop*), William Pawley (*Jim Haley*). Released by Fox Film Corp. 88m. Borzage won an Academy Award as best director.

AFTER TOMORROW (1932). Melodrama. A young couple's marriage is postponed again and again by hostile parents and financial difficulties. *Sc:* Sonya Levien (from a play by Hugh S. Stange and John Golden). *Ph:* James Wong Howe. *Art dir:* William Darling. *Ed:* Margaret Clancey. *Mus:* James Hanley. *With:* Charles Farrell (*Peter Piper*), Marian Nixon (*Sidney Taylor*), Minna Gombell (*Elsie Taylor*), William Collier, Sr. (*William Taylor*), Josephine Hull (*Mrs. Piper*), William Pawley (*Malcolm Jarvis*), Greta Granstedt, Ferdinand Munier, Nora Lane. Released by Fox

Film Corp. 79m.

YOUNG AMERICA (1932). Melodrama. A tough, orphaned youngster, thought to be a juvenile delinquent, goes straight and, through good deeds, redeems himself. *Sc:* William Conselman (from play by John Frederick Ballard). *Ph:* George Schneiderman. *Art dir:* Duncan Cramer. *Ed:* Margaret Clancey. *With:* Spencer Tracy (*Jack Doray*), Doris Kenyon (*Edith Doray*), Tommy Conlon (*Arthur Simpson*), Ralph Bellamy (*Judge Blake*), Beryl Mercer (*Grandma Beamish*), Sarah Padden (*Mrs. Taylor*), Robert Homans (*Patrolman Weems*), Raymond Borzage (*Nutty*), Dawn O'Day, Betty Jane Graham, Louise Beavers, Spec O'Donnell, William Pawley, Eddie Sturgis. Released by Fox Film Corp. 71m. Raymond Borzage is Frank's nephew.

A FAREWELL TO ARMS (1932). Melodrama. A cynical soldier discovers happiness in the midst of war when he falls in love with a nurse; separated from her, he deserts his outfit to find her. *Sc:* Benjamin Glazer and Oliver H. P. Garrett (from novel by Ernest Hemmingway). *Ph:* Charles Lang. *Art dir:* Roland Anderson and Hans Dreier. *Ed:* Otho Lovering. *With:* Helen Hayes (*Catherine Barkley*), Gary Cooper (*Lt. Frederick Henry*), Adolphe Menjou (*Major Rinaldi*), Mary Phillips (*Helen Ferguson*), Jack La Rue (*Priest*), Blanche Frederici, Henry Armetta, George Humbert, Fred Malatesta, Mary Forbes, Tom Ricketts, Robert Cautero, Gilbert Emery. Released by Paramount. 90m. The film was released with two endings—one based on Hemingway's original ending and another, happier one in which Catherine

recovers.

SECRETS (1933). Melodrama. A remake of Borzage's 1924 film. *Sc:* Frances Marion, Salisbury Field and Leonard Praskins (from play by Rudolf Besier and May Edginton). *Ph:* Ray June. *Ed:* Hugh Bennett. *With:* Mary Pickford (*Mary Marlowe*), Leslie Howard (*John Carlton*), C. Aubrey Smith (*Mr. Marlowe*), Blanche Frederici (*Mrs. Marlowe*), Doris Lloyd (*Susan Channing*), Herbert Evans (*Lord Hurley*), Ned Sparks (*Sunshine*), Allan Sears, Mona Maris, Lyman Williams, Virginia Grey, Ellen Johnson, Randolph Connelley, Huntley Gordon, Ethel Clayton, Bessie Barriscale, Theodore von Eltz. Released by United Artists. 85m.

MAN'S CASTLE (1933). Melodrama. During the Depression, a man feeds and shelters a homeless girl; though he falls in love with her, he fears the responsibilities and restrictions of marriage. *Sc:* Jo Swerling (story by Lawrence Hazard). *Ph:* Joseph August. *Ed:* Viola Lawrence. *Mus:* Frank Harling and Bakaleinikoff. *With:* Spencer Tracy (*Bill*), Loretta Young (*Trina*), Glenda Farrell (*Fay La Rue*), Walter Connolly (*Ira*), Arthur Hohl (*Bragg*), Marjorie Rambeau (*Flossie*), Dickie Moore (*Crippled Boy*). Released by Columbia Pictures. 75m.

LITTLE MAN, WHAT NOW? (1934). Melodrama. A young German couple marry during the postwar depression and struggle to make a living. *Sc:* William Anthony McGuire (from novel by Hans Fallada). *Ph:* Norbert Brodine. *Art dir:* Charles D. Hall. *Ed:* Milton Carruth. *Mus:* Arthur Kay. *With:* Margaret Sullavan (*Lämmchen*), Douglass

Montgomery (*Hans Pinneberg*), Alan Hale (*Jachman*), Catherine Doucet (*Mia Pinneberg*), Alan Mowbray (*Franz Schlüter*), Christian Rubb (*Puttbreese*), Fred Kohler (*Karl Goebbler, the Communist*), Mae Marsh (*His Wife*), De Witt Jennings, Muriel Kirkland, G. P. Huntley, Jr., Etienne Girardot, Hedda Hopper, Sarah Padden, George Meeker, Donald Haines, Bodil Rosing, Paul Fix. *Prod:* Carl Laemmle Jr. for Universal Pictures. 90m.

NO GREATER GLORY (1934). Melodrama. Two boys' clubs fight over a vacant lot and are drawn together by one boy's sacrifices. *Sc:* Jo Swerling (based on novel by Ferenc Molnar). *Ph:* Joseph August. *Ed:* Viola Lawrence. *Mus:* Louis Silvers. *With:* George Breakston (*Nemecsek*), Jimmy Butler (*Boka*), Jackie Searl (*Gereb*), Frankie Darro (*Feri Ato*), Donald Haines (*Csonakos*), Rolf Ernest (*Ferdie Pasztor*), Christian Rubb (*Watchman*), Ralph Morgan (*Nemecsek Sr.*), Lois Wilson (*mother*), Egon Brecher, Julius Molnar, Wesley Giraud, Beaudine Anderson, Samuel Hinds. Released by Columbia Pictures. 78m.

FLIRTATION WALK (1934). Musical comedy. A private in the army, in love with his commanding officer's daughter, goes to West Point to become an officer and a gentleman. *Sc:* Delmer Daves (story by Daves and Lou Edelman). *Ph:* Sol Polito and George Barnes. *Art dir:* Jack Okey. *Ed:* William Holmes. *Mus:* Allie Wrubel and Mort Dixon (dance numbers directed by Bobby Connolly). *With:* Dick Powell (*Dick "Canary" Dorcy*), Ruby Keeler (*Kit Fitts*), Pat O'Brien (*Sgt. Scrapper Thornhill*), Ross Alexander (*Oskie*), John Arledge (*Spike*), John

Eldredge (*Lt. Robert Biddle*), Henry O'Neill (*Gen. John Brent Fitts*), Guinn Williams (*Sleepy*), Frederick Burton, John Darrow, Glen Boles, Col. Tim Lonergan, Gertrude Keeler, Tyrone Power. *Prod:* Frank Borzage for Warner Bros.-First National. 97m.

LIVING ON VELVET (1935). Melodrama. Sole survivor of a plane crash that killed his father, mother and sister, a man thinks he lives on borrowed time and surrenders to the spirit of depression that that creates. *Sc:* Jerry Wald and Julius Epstein. *Ph:* Sid Hickox. *Art dir:* Robert Haas. *Ed:* William Holmes. *Mus:* Leo F. Forbstein. *With:* Kay Francis (*Amy Prentiss*), George Brent (*Terry Parker*), Warren William (*Gibraltar Pritcham*), Russell Hicks (*Major*), Maude Turner Gordon (*Mrs. Parker*), Sam Hinds (*Mr. Parker*), Martha Merrill (*Cynthia Parker*), Helen Lowell, Henry O'Neill, Edgar Kennedy. *Prod:* Edward Chodorov for Warner Bros.-First National. 80m.

STRANDED (1935). Melodrama. A girl working for the Traveler's Aid cures a tough engineer of his cynicism. *Sc:* Delmer Daves and Carl Erickson (story by Frank Wead and Ferdinand Reyher). *Ph:* Sid Hickox. *Art dir:* Anton Grot and Hugh Reticker. *Ed:* William Holmes. *With:* Kay Francis (*Lynn Palmer*), George Brent (*Mack Hale*), Patricia Ellis (*Velma Tuthill*), Donald Woods (*John Wesley*), Robert Barrat (*Stanislaus Janauschek*), Barton MacLane (*Sharkey*), Joseph Crehan, Mary Forbes, John Wray, Florence Fair, Frankie Darro, Ann Shoemaker, Mae Busch, Henry O'Neill, Joan Gay, Gavin Gordon. Released by Warner Bros.-First National.

SHIPMATES FOREVER (1935). Musical comedy. Young singer, descendant of a long line of admirals, opposes family tradition but enters Annapolis on a challenge and finally adjusts to the Navy. *Sc:* Delmer Daves. *Ph:* Sol Polito. *Art dir:* Robert M. Haas. *Ed:* William Holmes. *Mus:* Leo F. Forbstein (songs by Harry Warren and Al Dubin). *With:* Dick Powell (*Richard John Melville III*), Ruby Keeler (*June Blackburn*), Lewis Stone (*Admiral Melville*), Ross Alexander (*Sparks*), Eddie Acuff (*Slim*), Dick Foran (*Gifford*), John Arledge (*Coxswain*), Robert Light (*Ted Sterling*). A Cosmopolitan Production. Released by Warner Bros.-First National. 124m.

DESIRE (1936). Comedy. An American engineer falls in love with and reforms an international jewel thief. *Sc:* Edwin Justus Mayer, Waldemar Young and Samuel Hoffenstein (play by Hans Szekely and R. A. Stemmle). *Ph:* Charles Lang. *Art dir:* Hans Dreier and Robert Usher. *Ed:* William Shea. *Mus:* Frederick Hollander and Leo Robin. *With:* Marlene Dietrich (*Madeleine de Beaupré*), Gary Cooper (*Tom Bradley*), John Halliday (*Carlos Margoli*), William Frawley (*Mr. Gibson*), Ernest Cossart (*Aristide Duval*), Alan Mowbray (*Dr. Edouard Pauquet*), Effie Tilbury (*Aunt Olga*), Akim Tamiroff, Enrique Acosta, Alice Feliz. *Prod:* Ernst Lubitsch for Paramount Pictures. 99m.

HEARTS DIVIDED (1936). Melodrama. A Nineteenth century American girl from Baltimore falls in love with Napoleon's brother. *Sc:* Laird Doyle and Casey Robinson (from play by Rida Johnson Young). *Ph:* George Folsey. *Art dir:* Robert Haas. *Ed:* William Holmes. *Mus:* Harry Warren and Al Dubin. *With:* Marion Davies (*Betsy Patterson*), Dick Powell (*Jerome Bonaparte*), Charlie Ruggles (*Henry Ruggles*), Claude Rains (*Napoleon Bonaparte*), Edward Everett Horton (*John Hathaway*), Arthur Treacher (*Sir Harry*), Henry Stephenson (*Charles Patterson*), Clara Blandick, Halliwell Hobbes, John Larkin, Walter Kingsford, Etienne Girardot, Hattie McDaniels. *Prod:* Harry Joe Brown for Cosmopolitan Productions. Released by Warner Bros. 76m. Eighteen minutes were cut from the film between its Hollywood and New York previews.

GREEN LIGHT (1937). Melodrama. Doctor assumes the blame for a patient's death and dedicates himself to medical research. *Sc:* Milton Krims (from novel by Lloyd C. Douglas). *Ph:* Byron Haskins. *Art dir:* Max Parker. *Ed:* James Gibbons. *Mus:* Max Steiner (conducted by Leo F. Forbstein). *With:* Errol Flynn (*Dr. Newell Paige*), Anita Louise (*Phyllis Dexter*), Margaret Lindsay (*Francis Ogilvie*), Sir Cedric Hardwicke (*Dean Harcourt*), Walter Abel (*John Stafford*), Henry O'Neill (*Dr. Endicott*), Spring Byington (*Mrs. Dexter*), Erin O'Brien-Moore, Henry Kolker, Pierre Watkins, Granville Bates, Russell Simpson, Myrtle Stedman. *Prod:* Hal B. Wallis for Cosmopolitan Productions. Released by Warner Bros. 85m.

HISTORY IS MADE AT NIGHT (1937). Melodrama. A husband's demonic jealousy drives his wife to divorce him; he tries to keep her from framing her new lover with a crime he himself committed. *Sc:* Gene Towne and Graham Baker. *Ph:* Gregg Toland. *Ed:* Margaret Clancey. *With:* Charles Boyer

(*Paul Dumond*), Jean Arthur (*Irene Vail*), Leo Carrillo (*Cesare*), Colin Clive (*Bruce Vail*), Ivan Lebedeff (*Michael*), George Meeker, Lucian Prival, Georges Renavent, George Davies, Adele St. Mauer. *Prod:* Walter Wanger for United Artists. 97m.

THE BIG CITY (1937). Melodrama. A war between rival taxi companies threatens the happiness of a young cab driver and his foreign-born wife. *Sc:* Dore Schary and Hugo Butler (story by Norman Krasna). *Ph:* Joseph Ruttenberg. *Art dir:* Cedric Gibbons. *Ed:* Frederick Y. Smith. *Mus:* Dr. William Axt. *With:* Spencer Tracy (*Joe Benton*), Louise Rainer (*Anna Benton*), Charley Grapewin (*mayor*), Janet Beecher (*Sophie Sloane*), Eddie Quillan (*Mike Edwards*), Victor Varconi (*Paul Roya*), Oscar O'-Shea, Helen Troy, William Demarest, John Arledge, Irving Bacon, Guinn Williams, Regis Toomey, Edgar Dearing, Paul Harvey, Grace Ford, Alice White, Clem Bevans, Jack Dempsey, Jim Jeffries, Maxie Rosenbloom, Jim Thorpe. *Prod:* Norman Krasna for M-G-M. 80m. Re-titled THE SKYSCRAPER WILDERNESS.

THREE COMRADES (1938). Melodrama. The friendship and love of three war comrades and a girl give meaning to all their lives. *Sc:* F. Scott Fitzgerald and Edward Paramore (from novel by Erich Maria Remarque). *Ph:* Joseph Ruttenberg. *Art dir:* Cedric Gibbons. *Ed:* Frank Sullivan. *Mus:* Franz Waxman. *With:* Robert Taylor (*Erich Lohkamp*), Margaret Sullavan (*Pat Hollman*), Franchot Tone (*Otto Koster*), Robert Young (*Gottfried Lenz*), Guy Kibbee (*Alfons*), Lionel Atwill (*Franz Freuer*), Henry Hull (*Dr. Heinrich Becker*), George Zucco, Charley Grapewin, Monty Woolley, Spencer Charters, Sarah Padden. *Prod:* Joseph L. Mankiewicz for M-G-M. 100m.

THE SHINING HOUR (1938). Melodrama. A New York showgirl disrupts a Wisconsin farm family by marrying into it. *Sc:* Jane Murfin and Ogden Nash (from play by Keith Winter). *Ph:* George Folsey. *Art dir:* Cedric Gibbons. *Ed:* Frank E. Hull. *Mus:* Franz Waxman. *With:* Joan Crawford (*Olivia Riley*), Margaret Sullavan (*Judy Linden*), Robert Young (*David Linden*), Melvyn Douglas (*Henry Linden*), Fay Bainter (*Hanna Linden*), Allyn Joslyn (*Roger Q. Franklin*), Hattie McDaniels (*Belvedere*), Oscar O'Shea, Frank Albertson, Harry Barris. *Prod:* Joseph L. Mankiewicz for M-G-M. 76m.

MANNEQUIN (1938). Melodrama. A girl escapes grim Hester Street tenements by marrying a small time con man; then meets a shipping magnate who falls in love with her. *Sc:* Lawrence Hazard (story by Katherine Brush). *Ph:* George Folsey. *Ed:* Frederick Y. Smith. *Mus:* Edward Ward. *With:* Joan Crawford (*Jessie Cassidy*), Spencer Tracy (*John L. Hennessey*), Alan Curtis (*Eddie Miller*), Ralph Morgan (*Briggs*), Mary Phillips (*Beryl*), Oscar O'Shea ("*Pa*" *Cassidy*), Elizabeth Risdon (*Mrs. Cassidy*), Leo Gorcy (*Clifford*). *Prod:* Joseph L. Mankiewicz for M-G-M. 94m.

DISPUTED PASSAGE (1939). Melodrama. A cynical young doctor discovers there is more to medicine than mere science. *Sc:* Anthony Veiller and Sheridan Gibney (from novel by Lloyd C. Douglas). *Ph:* William C. Mellor. *Art dir:* Hans Dreier and Roland Anderson. *Ed:* James Smith. *Mus:* Frederick Hollander and John Leipold. *With:* Dorothy Lamour (*Audrey Hilton*), Akim Tamiroff (*Dr. "Tubby" Forster*), John Howard (*John Wesley Beaven*), Judith Barrett (*Winifred Bane*), William Collier, Sr. (*Dr. Cunningham*), Victor Varconi (*Dr. La Ferriere*), Gordon Jones (*Bill Anderson*), Keye Luke, Elizabeth Risdon, Gaylord Pendleton, Billy Cook, William Pawley, Z. T. Nyi, Philson Ahn. *Prod:* Frank Borzage and Harlan Thompson for Paramount Pictures. 90m.

I TAKE THIS WOMAN (1940). A doctor saves a girl from a ruinous love affair, changing her life and his own. *Dir:* W. S. Van Dyke. *Sc:* Charles MacArthur and James Kevin McGuinness. *Ph:* Harold Rosson. *Art dir:* Cedric Gibbons and Paul Groesse. *Mus:* Bronislau Kaper and Arthur Guttman. *With:* Hedy Lamarr (*Georgi Gregor*), Spencer Tracy (*Dr. Karl Decker*), Ina Claire (*Mme. Francesca*), Kent Taylor (*Phil*), Mona Barrie (*Jessica*), Louis Calhern (*Dr. Dureen*). Released by M-G-M. 97m. The film was begun by Josef von Sternberg (eighteen days) and completed by Borzage in 1938. Then it was re-shot by Van Dyke and released in 1940. Its working title was NEW YORK CINDERELLA.

STRANGE CARGO (1940). Melodrama. Convicts try to escape an island prison and to reach the mainland. *Sc:* Lawrence Hazard (from novel by Richard Sale). *Ph:* Robert Planck. *Art dir:* Cedric Gibbons. *Ed:* Robert J. Kern. *Mus:* Franz Waxman. *With:* Joan Crawford (*Julie*), Clark Gable (*Verne*), Ian Hunter (*Cambreau*), Peter Lorre (*M'sieu Pig*), Paul

THE MORTAL STORM: the last shot. The footsteps have been filled in with snow. Frame enlargement

Lukas (*Hessler*), Albert Dekker (*Moll*), J. Edward Bromberg (*Flaubert*), Eduardo Ciannelli (*Telez*), John Arledge (*Dufond*), Victor Varconi (*Fisherman*), Frederic Worlock (*Grideau*). *Prod:* Joseph L. Mankiewicz for M-G-M. 113m. The Legion of Decency originally gave the film a "C" rating, condemning it for its "irreverent use of Sacred Scriptures" and "lustful implications in dialogue and situation."

THE MORTAL STORM (1940). Melodrama. The rise of Fascism in Germany destroys a family. *Sc:* Claudine West, Anderson Ellis and George Froeschel (from novel by Phyllis Bottome). *Ph:* William Daniels. *Art dir:* Cedric Gibbons. *Ed:* Elmo Veron. *Mus:* Edward Kane. *With:* Margaret Sullavan (*Freya*

143

Roth), James Stewart (*Martin Breitner*), Robert Young (*Fritz Marberg*), Frank Morgan (*Prof. Roth*), Robert Stack (*Otto von Rohn*), Bonita Granville (*Elsa*), Irene Rich (*Mrs. Roth*), William T. Orr (*Erich von Rohn*), Maria Ouspenskaya (*Mrs. Breitner*), Gene Reynolds (*Rudi*), Russell Hicks, William Edmonds, Esther Dale, Dan Daily, Jr., Granville Bates, Thomas Ross, Ward Bond. *Prod:* Frank Borzage and Victor Saville (uncredited). Released by M-G-M. 100m.

FLIGHT COMMAND (1940–41). A cadet enters a famous naval flight squadron and struggles to win the respect of its members. *Sc:* Wells Root and Com. Harvey Haislip (story by Com. Haislip and John Sutherland). *Ph:* Harold Rosson. *Ed:* Robert J. Kern. *Mus:* Franz Waxman. *With:* Robert Taylor (*Alan Drake*), Ruth Hussey (*Lorna Gary*), Walter Pidgeon (*"Dusty" Rhodes*), Shepperd Strudwick (*Jerry Banning*), Red Skelton (*"Mugger" Martin*), Nat Pendleton (*"Spike" Knowles*), Dick Purcell (*"Stitchy" Payne*), William Tannen (*Freddy Townsend*), William Stelling, Stanley Smith, Addison Richards, Donald Douglas, Pat Flaherty, Marsha Hunt. *Prod:* J. Walter Ruben for M-G-M. 113m.

SMILIN' THROUGH (1941). Melodrama. Against the will of her guardian, an orphan falls in love with a man who proves to be the son of the murderer of her guardian's bride. *Sc:* Donald Ogden Stewart and John Balderson (from play by Jane Cowl and Jane Murfin). *Ph:* Leonard Smith (Technicolor). *Art dir:* Cedric Gibbons. *Ed:* Frank Sullivan. *Mus:* Herbert Stothart. *With:* Jeanette MacDonald (*Kathleen/Moonyean Clare*), Brian Aherne (*Sir John Carteret*), Gene

Raymond (*Kenneth/Jeremy Wayne*), Ian Hunter (*Rev. Owen Harding*), Frances Robinson (*Ellen*), Patrick O'Moore (*Willie*), Eric Lonsdale (*Charles*), Jackie Horner, David Clyde, Frances Carson, Ruth Rickaby. *Prod:* Victor Saville for M-G-M. 100m.

VANISHING VIRGINIAN (1942). An opponent of women's suffrage campaigns against a more liberal candidate in Virginia. *Sc:* Jan Fortune (from novel by Rebecca Yancey Williams). *Ph:* Charles Lawton. *Art dir:* Cedric Gibbons. *Ed:* James N. Newcom. *Mus:* David Snell and Lennie Hayton. *With:* Frank Morgan (*Robert Yancey*), Kathryn Grayson (*Rebecca Yancey*), Spring Byington (*Rosa Yancey*), Natalie Thompson (*Margaret Yancey*), Douglass Newland (*Jim Shirley*), Mark Daniels (*Jack Holden*), Elizabeth Patterson (*Grandma*), Juanita Quigley (*Caroline Yancey*), Scotty Beckett (*Joel Yancey*), Dickie Jones, Leigh Whipper, Louise Beavers, J. M. Kerrigan. *Prod:* Edwin Knopf for M-G-M. 97m.

SEVEN SWEETHEARTS (1942). A young man falls in love with one of seven daughters but can not marry her until the eldest daughter weds. *Sc:* Walter Reisch and Leo Townsend. *Ph:* George Folsey. *Art dir:* Cedric Gibbons. *Ed:* Blanche Sewell. *Mus:* Franz Waxman (songs by Walter Jurman, Paul Francis Webster, Burton Lane and Ralph Freed). *With:* Kathryn Grayson (*Billie Van Maaster*), Van Heflin (*Henry Taggert*), Marsha Hunt (*Regina*), Cecilia Parker (*Victor*), Peggy Moran (*Albert*), Mrs. Nugent (*Diana Lewis*), S. Z. Sakall (*Mr. Van Maaster*), Dorothy Morris (*Peter*), Frances Rafferty (*George*), Frances Raeburn (*Cornelius*), Carl Esmond, Michael Butler, Cliff Danielson, Donald Meek, Louise Beavers, William Roberts. *Prod:* Joe Pasternak for M-G-M. 98m.

STAGE DOOR CANTEEN (1943). Musical. Three hostesses from the Stage Door Canteen meet soldiers on leave and break the canteen's rules to date them. *Sc:* Delmer Daves. *Ph:* Harry Wild. *Art dir:* Hans Peters. *Ed:* Hal Kern. *Mus:* C. Bakaleinikoff. *With:* Cheryl Walker (*Eileen*), William Terry (*Dakota*), Marjorie Riordan (*Jean*), Lon McCallister (*California*), Margaret Early (*Ella Sue*), Michael "Sunset Carson" Harrison (*Texas*), Dorothea Kent (*Mamie*), Fred Brady (*Jersey*), Marion Shockley (*Lillian*), Patrick O'Moore (*Australian*), Ruth Roman, and dozens of Hollywood stars including Tallulah Bankhead, Katharine Hepburn, George Jessel, Ray Bolger. *Prod:* Sol Lesser for United Artists. 132m.

HIS BUTLER'S SISTER (1943). Comedy. A rich New Yorker falls in love with his butler's sister. *Sc:* Samuel Hoffenstein and Betty Reinhardt. *Ph:* Woody Bredell. *Art dir:* John B. Goodman and Martin Obzina. *Mus:* Charles Previn. *With:* Deanna Durbin (*Ann Carter*), Franchot Tone (*Charles Gerard*), Pat O'Brien (*Martin Murphy*), Akim Tamiroff (*Popoff*), Alan Mowbray (*Jenkins*), Walter Catlett (*Kalb*), Elsa Janssen, Evelyn Ankers, Frank Jenks, Sig Arno, Hans Conreid, Florence Bates, Andrew Tombes. *Prod:* Felix Jackson, Frank Borzage and Frank Shaw for Universal Pictures. 93m.

TILL WE MEET AGAIN (1944). Melodrama. A French nun leads a downed American aviator through German lines to freedom. *Sc:* Lenore Coffee (from play by Alfred Maury). *Ph:* Theodor Sparkuhl. *Art dir:* Hans Dreier and Robert Usher. *Ed:* Elmo Veron. *Mus:* David Buttolph. *With:* Ray Milland (*John*), Barbara Britton (*Sister Clothilde*), Walter Slezak (*Vitrey*), Lucille Watson (*Mother Superior*), Konstantin Shayne (*Major Krupp*), Vladimir Sokoloff (*Cabeau*), Marguerite D'Alvarez, Mona Freeman, William Edmunds, George Davis, Peter Helmess, John Wengraf. *Prod:* Frank Borzage for Paramount Pictures. 88m.

THE SPANISH MAIN (1945). Adventure. Pirate prevents girl from marrying his enemy, the governor of a Caribbean island, and falls in love with her himself. *Sc:* George Worthing Yates, Herman J. Mankiewicz and Aeneas Mackenzie (story by Aeneas Mackenzie). *Ph:* George Barnes (Technicolor). *Art dir:* Al D'Agostino. *Ed:* Ralph Dawson. *Mus:* Hanns Eisler and C. Bakaleinikoff. *With:* Paul Henreid (*Laurent Van Horn*), Maureen O'Hara (*Francisca*), Walter Slezak (*Don Alvarado*), Binnie Barnes (*Anne Bonny*), John Emery (*Bilay*), Barton MacLane (*Capt. Black*), J. M. Kerrigan (*Pillory*), Fritz Leiber, Nancy Gates, Jack LaRue, Mike Mazurki, Ian Keith, Victor Kilian, Curt Bois. *Prod:* Robert Fellows for RKO-Radio Pictures. 101m.

MAGNIFICENT DOLL (1946). Melodrama. Story of Dolly Madison's rejection of the cynical Aaron Burr for the idealistic James Madison. *Sc:* Irving Stone. *Ph:* Joseph Valentine. *Ed:* Ted J. Kent. *Mus:* H. J. Salter. *With:* Ginger Rogers (*Dolly*), David Niven (*Aaron Burr*), Burgess Meredith (*James Madison*), Horace McNally (*John Todd*), Peggy Wood (*Mrs. Payne*), Frances Williams (*Amy*), Robert Barrat (*Mr. Payne*), Grandon Rhodes (*Thomas Jefferson*). *Prod:* Jack H. Skirball and Bruce Manning for Hallmark Productions. Released by Universal Pictures. 95m.

I'VE ALWAYS LOVED YOU (1946). Melodrama. Young pianist falls in love with her maestro but marries another. *Sc:* Bordon Chase (story by Chase). *Ph:* Tony Gaudio (Technicolor). *Art dir:* Howard E. Johnson, John McCarthy, Jr. and Leanora Pierotti. *Ed:* Richard L. Van Enger. *Mus:* Walter Scharf (piano recordings by Artur Rubinstein). *With:* Philip Dorn (*Leopold Goronoff*), Catherine McLeod (*Myra Hassman*), William Carter (*George Sampter*), Maria Ouspenskaya (*Mme. Goronoff*), Felix Bressart (*Frederick Hassman*), Fritz Feld (*Nicholas*), Elizabeth Patterson (*Mrs. Sampter*), Vanessa Brown (*Porgy*), Lewis Howard (*Michael Severin*), Adele Mara, Gloria Donovan, Cora Witherspoon. *Prod:* Frank Borzage for Republic Pictures. 117m. This was Republic's first Technicolor film.

THAT'S MY MAN (1947). Melodrama. A gambler drifts away from his family but is brought back to them by his race horse, Gallant Man. *Sc:* Steve Fisher and Bradley King. *Ph:* Tony Gaudio. *Art dir:* James Sullivan. *Ed:* Richard L. Van Enger. *Mus:* Hans Salter and Cy Feuer. *With:* Don Ameche (*Joe Grange*), Catherine McLeod (*Ronnie*), Roscoe Karns (*Toby Gleeton*), John Ridgely (*Ramsey*), Kitty Irish (*Kitty*), Joe Frisco (*Willie Wagonstatter*), Gregory Marshall, Dorothy Adams, Frankie Darro, Hampton J. Scott, William B. Davidson, Joe Hernandez, Gallant Man. *Prod:* Frank Borzage for Republic Pictures.

104m.

MOONRISE (1949). Melodrama. Son of a man hung for murder kills another man in a fight and fears he has inherited bad blood. *Sc:* Charles Haas (from novel by Theodore Straus). *Ph:* John L. Russell. *Art dir:* John McCarthy Jr. and George Sawley. *Ed:* Harry Keller. *Mus:* William Lava ("The Moonrise Song" by Harry Tobias and William Lava). *With:* Dane Clark (*Danny Hawkins*), Gail Russell (*Gilly Johnson*), Ethel Barrymore (*Grandma*), Allyn Joslyn (*Clem Otis*), Rex Ingram (*Mose*), Henry Morgan (*Billy Scripture*), David Street (*Ken Williams*), Selena Royle (*Aunt Jessie*), Harry Carey, Jr., Irving Bacon, Lloyd Bridges, Phil Brown, Clem Bevans, Lila Leeds. *Prod:* Charles Haas for Republic Pictures. 90m.

CHINA DOLL (1958). Melodrama. Second World War transport pilot falls in love with Chinese servant girl, discovering love in the bleakness of war. *Sc:* Kitty Buhler (story by James Benson Nablo and Thomas F. Kelly). *Ph:* William H. Clothier. *Art dir:* Howard Richmond. *Ed:* Jack Murray. *Mus:* Henry Vars. *With:* Victor Mature (*Cliff Brandon*), Li Li Hua (*Shu-Jen*), Ward Bond (*Father Cairns*), Bob Mathias (*Phil Gates*), Stu Whitman (*Dan O'Neill*), Johnny Desmond (*Steve Hill*), Ken Perry (*Ernie Fleming*), Don Barry (*Hal Foster*), Danny Chang (*Ellington*), Steve Mitchell, Elaine Curtis, Ann McCrea, Ann Paige, Denver Pyle. *Prod:* Frank Borzage for Romina Productions. Released by United Artists. 88m.

THE BIG FISHERMAN (1959). Biblical spectacular. Love story of Near East prince and princess set against stories of

THE BIG FISHERMAN: Frank Borzage and Martha Hyer on the set

Christ's disciples, Simon and John the Baptist. *Sc:* Howard Estabrook and Rowland V. Lee (from novel by Lloyd C. Douglas). *Ph:* Lee Garmes (Panavision and Technicolor). *Art dir:* Julia Heron. *Ed:* Paul Weatherwax. *Mus:* Albert Ray Malotte and Joseph Gershenson. *With:* Howard Keel (*Simon-Peter*), Susan Kohner (*Princess Fara*), John Saxon (*Prince Voldi*), Martha Hyer (*Herodias*), Her-

bert Lom (*Herod-Antipas*), Ray Stricklyn (*Prince Deran*), Marian Seldes (*Princess Arnon*), Alexander Scourby (*David Ben-Zadok*), Beulah Bondi (*Hannah*), Jay Barney, Charlotte Fletcher, Mark Dana, Rhodes Reason, Henry Brandon, Brian Hutton. *Prod:* Rowland V. Lee for Centurion Films. Released by Buena Vista. 180m.

147

Edgar G. Ulmer

Edgar G. Ulmer, one of the least known, least seen and least appreciated of American directors, remains one of the greatest film-makers to emerge from the shadowy lower depths of Hollywood's "B" feature production industry in the Forties. One of his era's bleakest artists and one of *film noir*'s blackest visionaries, Ulmer today is all but forgotten, except by a handful of admirers and a score of detractors.

To most, Ulmer is a totally unknown or, at best, an obscure figure in film history. Since his career and the conditions under which he worked are somewhat unusual, a few facts about his life may help bring his obscurity into sharper focus and place his films in a context in which they can be better understood.

Like Erich von Stroheim, Josef von Sternberg, Fritz Lang, Billy Wilder and Otto Preminger, Ulmer was born in Vienna around the turn of the century (on September 17, 1904, to be exact). After studying architecture at the Academy of Arts and Sciences, he became, at the age of sixteen, a set designer for the legendary stage director, Max Reinhardt, at his Theater in der Josefstadt. There he met future film director F. W. Murnau. Ulmer also worked at this time in Berlin as set designer on films made there by Paul Wegener, Robert Wiene, Alexander Korda, Michael Curtiz (Kertész) and Mauritz Stiller. In 1923, Ulmer visited the United States with Reinhardt's play, "The Miracle," and designed some sets for Universal. In the same year he became one of Murnau's assistants (*Der letzte Mann,* 1924, and *Faust,* 1926) and worked with him on most of his American productions as assistant and set designer, uncred-

Opposite: Edgar G. Ulmer with the Blue Madonna, a gift from the Italians in 1948, taken in 1971 by Peter Bart ("New York Times"). Courtesy of Mrs. Ulmer

ited except for *Sunrise* (1927), until Murnau left the country in 1929 to make *Tabu*. After this long apprenticeship with Murnau—during which he worked with Cecil B. DeMille and also made dozens of two-reel westerns, Ulmer returned to Berlin to make his first feature, *Menschen am Sonntag* (1929), co-directed with Robert Siodmak. In 1930, Ulmer moved back to the U.S. where he worked, until 1933, both as art director at Metro-Goldwyn-Mayer and as stage designer for the Philadelphia Grand Opera Company. During the Franklin Delano Roosevelt administration, Ulmer was hired to make a number of foreign language films, mostly public-health documentaries, for various minority groups including Mexican-Americans, Orientals and American Indians.

Because Ulmer preferred to direct his own films and maintain control over their production, he worked for small-budget, independent production companies. Because producer interference caused delays on quickly made, small-budget films and made production costs prohibitive, Ulmer was free from such interference. As a result he achieved a control over his films that only a handful of Hollywood's greatest directors have enjoyed. Though many of his films look cheaply made, they all bear his signature.

Ulmer directed his first American film, *Damaged Lives*, in 1933 with independent financing. The next year, he wrote and directed one of his best known films, *The Black Cat,* based on an Edgar Allan Poe story, for Universal. After making *The Black Cat,* he worked in New York City producing and directing independently financed films for Jews, Ukrainians, Armenians, Blacks and other minority groups. In 1942, Ulmer returned to Hollywood with PRC (Producers' Releasing Corp.), a small but prolific company, where, under producer Leon Fromkess, he wrote and directed—at amazingly little cost and at an equally amazing rate—some of his best films: *Bluebeard* (1944), *Strange Illusion* (1945) and *Detour* (1946). After PRC folded in 1946, Ulmer founded his own short-lived company, Mid Century, and then went back to work for other small outfits. In the late Forties and early Fifties, Ulmer worked in Italy, Germany, Spain and the United States making films. In 1961, replacing Frank Borzage who became ill early in production, Ulmer re-wrote and finished *L'Atlantide*. His last film, *The Cavern,* was produced in Italy in 1965. Altogether, by his own count Ulmer has directed 128 films (though most filmographies list only about 35).

The quickness with which Ulmer worked, often completing a film a week (during one eleven-day period in 1960, he shot both *The Amazing Transparent Man* and *Beyond the Time Barrier*), and the cheapness of his productions in the Forties, occasionally costing as little as $20,000, makes the quality of his work all the more astounding. Though not all of Ulmer's films are of the highest quality, a surprising number of them are brilliant. *The Black Cat, Bluebeard, Strange Illusion, Detour, Ruthless* (1948), *The Naked Dawn* and *Murder Is My Beat* (1954) and *The Cavern* comprise a remarkably consistent *oeuvre* and reflect the depth of Ulmer's genius.

INITIATION INTO THE ULMER MYSTERIES

Little has been written about Ulmer. Luc Moullet, Ulmer's champion at "Cahiers du Cinéma" in the Fifties, parenthetically suggests some of the themes present in his work: "the great loneliness of man without God; the spiritual progression which leads from a yielding to Sin to the salvation of the soul, from the emptiness of existence to happiness, etc." ("Cahiers du Cinéma," Number 58, April 1956).

What is most important and interesting about Ulmer's characters, however, is neither their loneliness, though that is a factor, nor their spiritual progression (if, in fact, this does occur), but the nightmarish world that they inhabit. Ulmer's world, somewhat akin to Murnau's in its sensitivity to and assertion of abstract mystical forces that haunt its inhabitants, is an irrational one, governed more by crazy nightmare than by any coldly mechanical sense of fate. Ulmer's characters do not struggle against any externally imposed chain of events; rather, they are the powerless prisoners of an irrational series of experiences that they can neither understand nor control. Placed in an environment that answers reason with nightmare, their actions gradually become more inconsistent and more chaotic. Repeatedly surrendering themselves to their intuitive but irrational impulses, they lose control over their actions and their environment. Ultimately, Ulmer's characters exist only to suffer passively whatever happens to them.

The world around Ulmer's characters has no fixity and is incomprehensible. Ulmer's world, like Poelzig's (Karloff's) house in *The Black Cat,* stands upon a battlefield, is surrounded by a graveyard of the soldiers who died there and is undermined with dynamite. As one character, remarking on the presence of the dynamite, points out, "the slightest mistake by one of us could cause the destruction of all." Ulmer's characters, living on the brink of insanity, constantly run the risk of making that one mistake and of unleashing fantastically chaotic forces that will hound them to their own destruction.

One of the images that Ulmer frequently uses to express the paralysis of his characters by their environment is that of a drowning man. At the end of *Ruthless,* Vendig (Zachary Scott) and Buck (Sydney Greenstreet), each desperately choking the other, sink beneath the surface of the dark waters outside Vendig's mansion. Killed by a man he had earlier ruined in a business deal, Vendig drowns quite literally under the weight of his past sins. Like the drowning of Gaston Morel (John Carradine) at the end of *Bluebeard,* Vendig's death becomes a means of atonement for his past, and the water functions as a retributive force. Ulmer's Old Testament morality observes a strange logic: Vendig's rise in the world begins when he saves Martha from drowning; his ascent continues when he meets Susan, whose relatives are important financiers, after he wins a swim meet; it is only fitting that his death also comes through the agency of water. Ephraim Poster (Louis Hayward) in *The Strange Woman* (1946) has an intense fear of water and of drowning. We first see him as a child when Jenny, who years later marries Ephraim's father, sadistically pushes him into a stream and tries to drown him. Later, forced to accompany his father on a canoe trip through rough water, Ephraim overturns the boat and, terrified for his own life, struggles with his father over the support of a floating bucket and inadvertently drowns him. Ephraim's paralysing fear of the water finds its visual expression in his helplessness as he is caught in the swift current. Though Ephraim does not drown, his guilt over his father's death drives him to suicide.

The powerlessness of the trapped characters in *The Cavern* is epitomised by Ulmer in the death of Lt. Carter (Peter L. Marshall), a Canadian airman who drowns trying to find a way out of the cave which gives the film its title. His watery death is neither a punishment for past wrongdoing, nor a reflection of any paralysis by his inner fears. His "innocence" makes his death an even greater symbol for Ulmer's vision of fallen man. Man, in the Ulmer world, lives under the shadow of Original Sin, condemned by his very humanity. Anyone who tries to escape the nightmarish world he inhabits only meets frustration and remains totally at the mercy of forces stronger than himself which carry him to his death.

UNDERGROUND U.F.A.

The world around Ulmer's characters, both their physical environment and the events they experience, renders them its powerless prisoners. The archetypal Ulmerian situation consists of one or more characters helplessly trapped in a hostile, unfamiliar setting. In some films this entrapment is figurative, reflecting more a psychological than a physical constraint; in others, its literalness enriches the complexity of the situation by providing a visual metaphor for the abstract idea. In *Detour,* for example, Vera (Ann Savage) keeps Al Roberts (Tom Neal) prisoner in a shabby, rented apartment and forces him, more through a manipulation of Roberts's own fear and guilt than through physical force, to maintain the identity of the man he accidentally killed. At one point, Ulmer tracks in on Roberts and Vera from outside their window, conveying their entrapment through the framing window and its barrier of glass.

In other films, Ulmer entombs his characters in a subterranean world, burying them alive beneath the ground. The cold, modern architecture of Poelzig's house in *The Black Cat,* deceptively orderly in design with its bright open spaces and functionally geometric lines, stands over a dark cellar that contains a gallery of glass-encased dead women and rooms filled with medieval devices of torture. Beneath the surface logic and clarity of Poelzig's house lies its demonic inversion, the mysterious cellar in which he locks Peter Allison (David Manners), the film's helpless hero. In *Bluebeard,* the puppeteer is forced by a past trauma to kill again and again as he relives an earlier tragedy. Ulmer's *décor* echoes the dark, abstract forces that motivate the character: after one murder, we follow him down into the Parisian sewers into which he dumps his victims. The underground setting works as a visual metaphor for the character's psychological interment in a horrible past he continues to re-enact.

The subterranean, futuristic civilisation that Major Allison (Robert Clarke) discovers in *Beyond the Time Barrier* (1960) holds him prisoner in a more literal way. The survivors of a cosmic plague that left them sterile, the inhabitants of this underground world are doomed to extinction; though they are still alive, their subterranean entombment creates an atmosphere that suggests their living death. Their only hope lies in preventing Allison's escape and in mating him to Trirene (Darlene Tompkins), their sole non-sterile citizen.

Allison's accidental entry into this strange world makes him a victim of its plots and intrigues and a helpless subject of its laws. He remains powerless and his actions seem ineffectual. He appears hypnotised by this alien world and unable to break free of it. Like the explosions that destroy Poelzig's and Verdegast's universe at the end of *The Black Cat,* only the self-destruction of this world—seen in the riots of the mutants at the end of *Time Barrier*—makes escape from its grip possible.

In *The Cavern,* seven characters take refuge from an aerial bombardment in an underground Second World War supply dump, and are trapped in it when the retreating Italian army blows up its entrance to keep its munitions from falling into enemy hands. Unlike Ulmer's underground settings in his earlier films, the cavern functions less as a tomb or prison, although it is both, than as an environment of unfathomable, overwhelming mystery within which the characters' gestures and actions can only prove futile. When the characters first realise they have been locked in the cavern, Ulmer cuts to static shots of giant pillars formed by the joining of stalactites and stalagmites and, zooming in on them, suggests the mystical power this underground setting holds over its inhabitants. In their attempts at escape the characters try to master the cave's winding passageways and labyrinthine structure but fail again and again. Lt. Carter vainly tunnels into the roof of another cavern; then, he and Kramer (John Saxon) dam up an underground stream and follow its bed but find that it feeds into a larger stream that they cannot block without flooding the whole cave. Later, when the General (Brian Aherne) reads "Genesis" aloud, Ulmer cuts from close-ups of the listening characters to long shots of the cavern itself, equating the mystery of the Creation to that of the cavern and relating its inhabitants' own unspoken feelings to this larger mystery. Ulmer's editing and his use of the "Genesis" passage suggest his characters' new awareness of and sympathy with their setting and, at the same time, establish the cave's timelessness: we and Ulmer's characters intuitively feel the mystery of the Creation from which the cave dates and sense that of the Apocalypse until which it will endure.

THE FILMS: THE BLACK CAT

Ulmer frequently builds his films around the entry of innocent, uncomprehending characters into a decadent or corrupt world that is moving slowly but inevitably towards its own destruction. Finding themselves in this world, Ulmer's innocents are unable to resist its evil, become entangled in the deadly web spun by its inhabitants, and almost share their fate.

In *The Black Cat*, Peter and Joan (Jacqueline Wells) Allison, a newly married couple, become the passive victims of whatever environment they enter. Ulmer introduces them in the compartment of a train. When Verdegast (Bela Lugosi) enters their compartment, the strangeness of his manner and the intensity of his looks transform their environment. His presence on the train gives its journey a moral dimension that the Allison's mundane honeymoon lacks. We sense that Verdegast is going somewhere to do something: as the train reaches its destination, Ulmer dissolves from a close-up of Verdegast demonically proclaiming that after fifteen years in prison, "I have returned," to a shot of the train, its two headlights as intense as Verdegast's eyes, as it pulls into the station. The importance of his journey overwhelms that of his travelling companions, and, like the train they share, carries them along in its mysterious progress.

The Allisons, to borrow Verdegast's term, become "mediumistic" victims of their environment, vehicles for all the intangible forces in operation around them. Their imprisonment in Poelzig's house makes them helpless spectator-participants in the mortal struggle

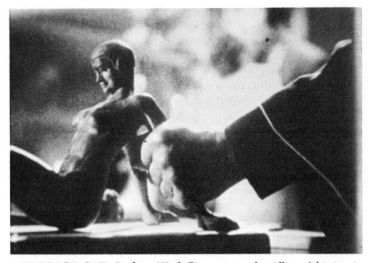

THE BLACK CAT: Poelzig (Karloff) reacts to the Allisons' kissing in the background by grabbing the statue in foreground. Frame enlargement

between Poelzig and Verdegast. They have no more control over or understanding of the situation than the chess pieces used by Poelzig and Verdegast to determine the Allisons' fate. Their environment—not only the house but the insane battle between Poelzig and Verdegast that takes place in it—becomes a nightmare from which they cannot awaken.

More interested in mental than physical experience, Ulmer concentrates not on actions but on reactions. In one scene, he pulls focus from the Allisons kissing in the background to Poelzig, reflexively grasping the arm of a bronze nude in the foreground as he watches them. At the end of the film, as Verdegast flays Poelzig alive, Ulmer cuts from shots of Poelzig's manacled hands to the shadows of the action projected on the cellar wall and to Joan, screaming as she is forced to watch this torture. The indirectness with which Ulmer presents the action conveys its psychological intensity; by building the scene around Joan's reaction to it, Ulmer transforms physical reality into traumatic mental experience. *The Black Cat* focuses not on particular characters or events but on a pattern of reactions to events. What results is an intricately constructed series of moral and psychological encounters too mysterious for the Allisons or us ever to understand. We both remain an uncomprehending audience to a great yet inscrutable drama.

BLUEBEARD

The sympathetic villain of *Bluebeard*, one of Ulmer's most romantic films, is driven to kill by forces neither he nor the audience can understand. Like the scorpion that stings and drowns with the frog that ferries him across a river in Orson Welles's *Mr. Arkadin*, Gaston Morel (John Carradine) becomes a victim of his own nature. Against his own will he nearly strangles the girl he loves; he then falls to his death from a Parisian rooftop into the Seine below.

The film's tragic atmosphere and the emotionally sympathetic nature of its central character's actions are due in part to Ulmer's use of a performance of Gounod's "Faust," which provides us with a romantic, literary metaphor and an expressionistically cinematic one (Murnau's *Faust*), through which we can understand Morel's behaviour. A puppeteer by profession, Morel invites the modiste Lucille (Jean Parker) and her friends to a puppet performance of "Faust" in a park. Tracking in through the audience up to the small stage, and cutting in to close-ups of the puppets, Ulmer gives the Faust story such an immediacy and dramatic force that it dominates the subsequent action. The performance is so vivid and the puppets appear so real that their romantic story remains in the back of our minds throughout the film. Morel, akin to Faust, is forced to continue painting to pay off LaMarté, his Mephistopheles, and falls in love with Lucille, his Marguerite, whose sister he later kills.

During the performance, Ulmer pans up from the wooden puppets to the characters manipulating them, complicating the Faust metaphor with one of his own: his characters, like lifeless dolls, are motivated by unseen puppeteers, forces over which they have no control. In a flashback near the end of the film, Morel tells Lucille

BLUEBEARD: Marguerite in the puppet performance of Gounod's "Faust." All Ulmer's characters are puppet-like. Frame enlargement

BLUEBEARD: Ulmer tilts his camera during Gaston Morel's (John Carradine) flashback confession to record the traumatic nature of the experience. Frame enlargement

of his first murder. In a moment of artistic insanity, he killed a model whom he had saved from death, loved and painted, and who later betrayed his idealised vision of her. Ulmer stages the flashback on expressionistic, Caligari-like sets and shoots it with tilted camera angles. The craziness with which the flashback is shot reflects the irrationality of the forces that dictate Morel's actions in the present. Like the tilted-angle, superimposition dream sequences in *Daughter of Dr. Jekyll* (1957), the flashback reflects the mystical power of a traumatic mental experience that has stunned the action of Ulmer's characters and made them the prisoners of their own nightmares.

STRANGE ILLUSION

Like Gaston Morel in *Bluebeard,* many of Ulmer's characters resemble marionettes: they seem to be manipulated by some mysterious, invisible presence. In the Hamletesque *Strange Illusion,* Ulmer
creates, through an oracular nightmare, a supernatural bond between the dead Judge Cartwright and his puppet-like son, Paul
(James Lydon). After he wakes up from a traumatic nightmare in
which he foresees the intrusion as "father" of an "unscrupulous
impostor" in his family, Paul seems possessed by his father's spirit.
The next morning Paul receives a letter, left in trust for him by his
father before his mysterious death, asking him to guard his mother
and sister from those who might take advantage of them. He returns
home immediately and discovers that his mother has become interested in a man. His paranoid suspicion of his mother's would-be
fiancé, Brett Curtis (Warren William) and his eventual identification of Curtis as Claude Barrington, one of the men responsible for
his father's death, are treated by Ulmer as inspired by the dead
judge from beyond the grave.

When Paul, suspicious of Curtis, reads about Barrington in his
father's files, Ulmer slowly pans from Paul, at his father's desk,
past several objects in his father's study to a portrait of his father
hanging on the wall. It is as if the camera, aware of the mysterious
psychological link between Paul and his father, were tracing to its
origin the invisible lines of force that possess Paul and pull the
strings that manipulate him.

As Paul's original dream starts to come true, his increasing suspicions of Brett Curtis make his own behaviour—especially his
fainting spells—appear neurotic to those around him. Only by
proving his suspicions and thwarting Barrington's schemes does
Paul exorcise his father's demonic spirit and regain his own sanity.

The dreams that open and close *Strange Illusion* make explicit the film's concern for the psychological purgation of its central character. Using a melodrama invested with psychological overtones as a vehicle for this process, Ulmer works Paul's nightmare through in the "real" world, equating real and imagined experience. Ulmer's profoundly unsettling justification of Paul's paranoia affirms the existence and validity of a level of irrational experience that overwhelms all other experiences.

Ulmer's *mise-en-scène* in *Strange Illusion* roots itself not in logic, as Eric Rohmer's does, nor in the physical world, as Howard Hawks's does, but in the abstract, supernatural forces that control the minds of his characters. Ulmer's camera movements reveal a sympathetic sensitivity to the irrational forces that surround his characters. At the beginning of the film, a tracking shot through the woods to the edge of a lake—an oblique quote from Murnau's *Sunrise*—diverges from, then meets Mac, the game warden, who is bringing a letter to Paul from his dead father, bearing a warning that strangely coincides with Paul's earlier nightmare. Ulmer's camera, in tune with these larger, inexplicable forces, seems to follow an invisible path through the woods to its destination and remains responsive to a mystical level of experience of which neither his characters nor his plot seem to be aware.

DETOUR

The bleakness of *Detour* qualifies it for pre-eminence in the cinema of fear, paranoia and insanity, alongside such classics as Samuel Fuller's *Shock Corridor* (1963), Andre de Toth's *Day of the Outlaw* (1959) and Nicholas Ray's *Bigger Than Life* (1956). More than any other Ulmer film, *Detour* draws its central character into a fog-filled world from which escape is never even a distant possibility; Al Roberts (Tom Neal) embarks on a journey that destroys his identity and his will and that can only end in his death.

DETOUR: during his flashback, Roberts dreams of Sue (Claudia Drake) and her eventual success as a singer. Frame enlargement

The film begins at the end of its major action with Roberts's arrival at a Las Vegas diner. A record on the phonograph reminds him of the beginning of his journey and, as he thinks back, the lights in the diner dim and the camera tracks in to a close-up of his face, transforming the story he tells us into mental experience. His cross-country journey, because of the flashback and the constant intrusion of his voice-over narrative, becomes more psychological than real; we always remain aware of his reactions to what is happening to him. The events that take place, especially Haskell's

163

accidental death, become dream-like experiences he re-lives again and again, as in the dream montage that haunts his sleep in the motel he stops at after Haskell's death.

The cynicism of Roberts's outlook before his involvement with Haskell turns back upon itself later. By perceiving and reacting to his experiences sceptically and fatalistically, Roberts makes the action fatalistic. In the middle of his story, he philosophises: "That's life! Whichever way you turn, Fate sticks out its foot to trip you." Roberts's hard-boiled cynicism and subjective perception of the action create a weird sympathy between himself and the nightmarish

DETOUR: Ulmer pulls focus from Roberts (Tom Neal) to the image of the dead Vera (Ann Savage) in the mirror to convey Roberts's mental state

world around him that binds him to its logic, not his own. He becomes its prisoner, caught up helplessly in its flow like a man in a dream.

Later in the film, to keep Vera (Ann Savage)—who knows of Haskell's death—from calling the police, Roberts accidentally strangles her. Ulmer's subjective camera shows Roberts's mental process as he looks around the room at the objects that tie him to Vera's murder. It presents him as a passive reactor to the experience. Recording the psychological weight of Roberts's experience and reflecting the blurred focus of the crazy world he inhabits, Ulmer, in one continuous take, moves in and out of focus on various objects in the room. This visual punctuation of Roberts's perceptions draws us into his insanity, forcing us to share his shock at what has happened. His world loses what little clarity and fixity it had, and he is driven to the state of living death in which we initially find him. Roberts's mental journey has brought him nowhere. He remains in a perpetual state of limbo, stranded without an identity between nowhere and nowhere.

RUTHLESS

Ruthless, Ulmer's *Citizen Kane,* analyses the rise to a position of power and wealth of Horace Vendig (Zachary Scott) in a flashback structure which, like that in *Detour,* measures Vendig's success psychologically in terms of the mental and emotional anguish it has cost him.

The film begins with the arrival of Vic (Louis Hayward), Vendig's childhood friend and later business partner, and his girl friend Mallory (Diana Lynn) at Vendig's mansion for a ceremony in which he gives his fortune away to a peace organisation. Cutting from long shots of Vic's car winding along a road through the night towards Vendig's mansion to close-ups of its occupants—Mallory is questioning Vic about Vendig—Ulmer equates their literal journey with a more figurative investigation of the past, revealing his concern for abstract exposition of characters by relating them to their larger journey through their environment.

After the ceremony, Vendig sends for Vic and Mallory and talks with them in his study. Mallory's uncanny resemblance to Martha, the first casualty of Vendig's destructive ruthlessness, paralyses him. He starts to light a cigarette but stops in mid-gesture, remembering, through a flashback, his relationship with Martha. A reel and a half later, when the flashback ends, Ulmer returns us to Vendig frozen in the same gesture, suggesting Vendig's powerlessness in the face of his own past. It is as if he becomes an audience to his own life, as unable to change it as he is to explain it.

In spite of the film's attempts at narrative exposition, the backgrounds against which this exposition takes place only reaffirm the obscurity of Vendig's motivations. After saving Martha from drowning, young Vendig sits at home, wrapped in a blanket, as one of his mother's piano students plays an exercise off-screen in the background. Later, he visits his father, divorced from his mother, in his waterfront bar and restaurant. As they talk, the fish in a wall aquarium in the background dominate them. In both scenes, the backgrounds mystify more than they explain young Vendig's actions. As he moves through time from background to background, Vendig grows more irrational and mysterious. We never know what he really wants or feels; we only sense a strange tension between him and the world around him. The unseen forces that urge him through these backgrounds remain as mysterious as those that drive Roberts in *Detour* towards his own destruction.

Mallory's fascination with Vendig's hypnotic personality gradually draws her into his obsessive world. Her initial interest in him entangles her in a labyrinth of mystery and confusion from which only Vendig's death releases her. *Ruthless*, like *Kane*, ends with a reaffirmation of its initial mystery. As the tide carries the bodies of Vendig and Buck (Sydney Greenstreet) out to sea, we realise, along with Mallory, that Vendig's life, like his death, was governed by forces over which he had no control. The key to his mystery remains lost with his body in the depths of the dark ocean.

MURDER IS MY BEAT

Ulmer's narratives, unlike Hawks's, are characteristically disjointed; he introduces characters and settings without establishing their identity or location; transitions from scene to scene often appear chaotic and confused. In *Isle of Forgotten Sins* (1943), for example, we never know where the island is located. As in so many of his other settings, his characters are placed in a world in limbo. The introductory shot of Burke shows the distorted reflection of his face in a mirror as he shaves. The first shots of Clancy (John Carradine) show him strapped to his bunk, for reasons that the subsequent action never fully explains. Ulmer introduces us to situations and characters without warning. The frequency and consistency of his narrative lapses give them thematic significance: whether it is intentional or not, Ulmer's narrative discontinuity becomes symbolic of the forces of disorder and destruction that dominate his artistic universe. Ulmer reverses the practice of most directors who give their audience as much information or more than they give their characters, creating a dramatic irony that complicates the audience's responses to the action. Ulmer instead presents us with anonymous characters involved in actions we do not fully understand, establishing an atmosphere of confusion that reflects a nightmarish vision of the universe.

Murder Is My Beat begins with a long shot of a car driving down a highway. A close-up introduces us to the car's driver, Bert (Robert Shayne), but does not explain who he is, or where he is going, or

MURDER IS MY BEAT: Ray (Paul Langton) tracks Eden Lane to a
mountain cabin. Frame enlargement

why. The car pulls into a motel. Bert gets out, steals up to one of
the motel cabins and looks into its window. Through the window
we see Ray (Paul Langton), lying fully dressed and awake on a
bed. Ray's introduction, like Bert's, tells us nothing about him; it
establishes only his position in space. Bert breaks through the door
and fights with Ray until Ray recognises him and gives himself up.
It is only then that an expository flashback reveals that Ray, a police
detective, has been investigating a murder for Bert, who is his
immediate superior. Ulmer's visual introduction of characters and
situations before he establishes their narrative significance creates a

sense of mystery and disorder that colours the seemingly logical exposition that follows. When Ray traces the murder suspect, Eden Lane (Barbara Payton), to a mountain cabin and opens the cabin door to find her waiting there, Ulmer thrusts us into another narratively disjointed situation in which neither we nor Ray realise that Eden thinks she has only injured and not killed Frank Dean. Though Eden knows less than we know, we do not realise this until, later in the film, she innocently asks how badly hurt Dean was.

Parallel to this narrative confusion is a chaotic visual style that repeatedly changes the characters' positions in space by viewing them first from one angle, then from another totally different one. Discontinuous editing—for example the geographically dislocating close-up shot of the charred corpse that we see when Ray arrives at the scene of the crime—prevents us both from seeing the wholeness of an action or situation and from logically relating one character or detail to another. The effect of Ulmer's cutting in general is to isolate objects or characters from one another and from their surroundings, to take them out of space and time in order to expose them as abstract entities and to present them as iconographic ingredients in a larger experience that shrouds the characters in mystery. Ulmer's editing shows us that he is less interested in telling a story than in subjecting us, along with his characters, to the disordered universe he creates. This enables us to share his characters' muddled perceptions of their world, tying us to their irrationality.

While escorting Eden to prison on a train, Ray, who feels uneasy about the case, stares at her. As he begins to doubt her guilt, Ulmer cuts rhythmically from interior close-ups of Ray to exterior medium shots of the train speeding forward through the night. The disjointed cutting reflects Ray's uncertainty and, at the same time, relates his inner doubts to the journey of the train through space. Both the fragmented temporal structure of the film—its flashback form—and the visual confusion underlying the shooting of each scene deprive Ulmer's characters of their stability in space and of their reason, plunging them into an anarchic world of doubt and confusion.

ULMER'S CHARACTERS

It is pointless to question the motivation of Ulmer's characters. Roberts's decision in *Detour* to run away first from Haskell's death, then from Vera's has its logic only in the obscure nature of guilt itself. Vendig's treachery in *Ruthless,* though at first explicable as a means of bettering himself, of acquiring more money or power, seems finally, because of his dissatisfaction with what he gets, a totally irrational impulse. Similarly, the self-centred actions of Jenny (Hedy Lamarr) in *The Strange Woman,* which destroy both the men who love her and herself, have no logical motivation beyond her profound yearning for what she cannot have.

Ulmer's women in particular often appear to be mysteriously motivated and act irrationally. At times, they seem drawn by nothing but the force of evil itself. Fascinated and hypnotised, like Joan Allison in *The Black Cat,* they almost become its victims. The attraction of Maria (Betta St. John) to the outlaw Santiago (Arthur Kennedy) in *The Naked Dawn,* Mallory's interest in Vendig in *Ruthless,* the love of Paul's sister and mother for Curtis in *Strange Illusion,* Lucille's *amour fou* for her puppeteer in *Bluebeard,* reflect the paradoxical affinity in Ulmer's world between innocence and evil, an affinity that in each case ultimately results in that world's self-destruction.

Once Ulmer's characters acknowledge the existence of inexplicable and uncontrollable forces in the world, these forces are gradually reinforced and magnified by the characters' perceptions of them until the characters actually become their prisoners. In *Strange Illusion,* Paul's danger increases with his suspicions; Ulmer suggests this visually by locking him in Professor Muhlbach's asylum. In *The Cavern,* the characters' original sense of entrapment in the cave grows with each failure to find a way out of it. Hans, the German soldier, eventually finds a way out of the cave. But above ground he is shot by members of the Italian Resistance and dies before he can tell the others how to escape. After repeated failures, the characters struggle not so much to discover a way out as to maintain their sanity. All their logical and orderly attempts to escape fail. It is only a final, pathetic act of insanity—the General suicidally sets off an explosion which frees the others—that breaks the *décor*'s mysterious grip over them.

The inability of Ulmer's characters to control their environment, mirrored in their failure to control their own actions toward any purpose other than their self-destruction or self-punishment, indicates a deep-seated pessimism underlying all of Ulmer's work. Yet his characters' search, in the midst of this bleakness, for some positive value or absolute truth in their worlds makes them tremendously sympathetic. We sympathise even with his villains—with Vendig in *Ruthless* searching his past for a lost love, with Jenny in *The Strange Woman* looking for happiness. Ulmer's direction reveals great sensitivity to and sympathy for his characters' feelings. For example, when Paul and his mother discuss her loneliness and proposed marriage in *Strange Illusion,* their feeling for one another almost breaks the grip of the forces that control them (the judge and Curtis, respectively). In *Bluebeard,* Morel's affection for Lucille briefly purges him of the demon that haunts him. Vera's consumptive coughs and loneliness in *Detour* elicit a sympathetic, human response from Roberts—yet neither character can escape from the course of action to which he is committed.

Ulmer's irrational universe nearly drives some characters, like Al Roberts, insane. Yet Roberts, finally initiated into the mysteries of his world, begins to understand its irrationality a bit better. At the end of *Detour,* as he walks off alone into the night, he thinks about what has happened to him and wonders what his life would have been like if things had been different: "But there's one thing I don't have to wonder about. I know. Someday a car will stop to pick me up that I never thumbed. Yes. Fate, or some mysterious force, can put the finger on you or me for no good reason at all."

Ulmer's characters are pitifully weak. His plots often contain wide gaps in narrative continuity. Yet his visual style, as Jean Domarchi in "Cahiers #58" and Andrew Sarris in "The American Cinema" point out, never falters. In tune with a mystical level of experience, Ulmer seems to understand, with a certainty and sureness that is rare in the cinema, the invisible forces that make his characters' world a nightmare.

From the title credits of THE CARAVAN, Ulmer's last film

EDGAR G. ULMER Filmography*

Edgar George Ulmer was born in Vienna on September 17, 1904 and died September 30, 1972. After studying at the Academy of Arts and Sciences in Vienna, he acted and designed sets for Max Reinhardt's Josefstadt Theater. He came to the United States in 1923 as set decorator of Reinhardt's play, "The Miracle." Between 1924 and 1930 Ulmer assisted F. W. Murnau, whom he met through Reinhardt, on a number of his films (*Der letzte Mann, Tartuffe, Faust, Sunrise, Four Devils, City Girl* and *Tabu*). During this period, Ulmer co-directed *Menschen am Sonntag* (1929) in Germany with Robert Siodmak. Ulmer directed his first American film, *Damaged Lives*, in 1933 and, after the success of *The Black Cat* (1934), independently produced and directed a number of foreign language, minority-group films in New York and New Jersey. In 1942, Ulmer joined P.R.C. (Producer's Releasing Corporation) and, under the supervision of Leon Fromkess, became one of their top directors. At P.R.C. he also worked on the scripts and stories of Arthur Ripley's *Prisoner of Japan* (1942), William Nigh's *Corregidor* (1943) and Sam Newfield's *Danger! Women at Work* (1943). In the Fifties and Sixties, Ulmer directed films in Mexico, Italy, Spain, Germany and the United States. Ulmer's

---

* Material in this filmography is based on information contained in Luc Moullet's biofilmography in "Cahiers du Cinéma," no. 58, April 1956 and information supplied by Mrs. Ulmer.

wife, Shirley, assisted on the scripts of all his films and his daughter, Arianne Ulmer Cipes, a graduate of the Royal Academy of Dramatic Arts in London, appeared in a number of his films (including *The Strange Woman, The Pirates of Capri* and *Beyond the Time Barrier*). By his own count, Ulmer directed 128 films. This filmography lists 39 of those.

MENSCHEN AM SONNTAG (1929). Pseudo-documentary. A typical Sunday in the lives of five Berliners. *Co-dir:* Robert Siodmak. *Sc:* Billy Wilder, Robert Siodmak, Edgar G. Ulmer, and Fred Zinnemann (from idea by Kurt Siodmak). *Ph:* Eugen Schüfftan. *With:* Brigitte Borchert, Christl Ehlers, Annie Schreyer, Wolfgang von Waltershausen, Erwin Splettstösser. Released by Filmstudio. 59m. Its English language title is PEOPLE ON SUNDAY.

DAMAGED LIVES (1933). Clinical melodrama. A young couple become victims of syphilis, undergo treatment and become case studies for a clinical discussion of the disease. *Sc:* Donald Davis and Edgar G. Ulmer (clinical supervision by Dr. Gordon Bates). *Ph:* Al Sieglar. *With:* Diane Sinclair (*Joan*), Lyman Williams (*Donald Bradley*), George Irving (*Mr. Bradley*), Almeda Fowler (*Mrs. Bradley*), Jason Robards (*Dr. Hall*), Marceline Day (*Mrs. Hall*), Charlotte Merriam (*Alyce*), Murray Kinnell, Harry Meyers. Released by Weldon Pictures Corp. 60m. After some trouble with the New York State Board of Censors, the film's sponsors, The American Social Hygiene Society, appealed their decision and won the right to exhibit the film.

THE BLACK CAT (1934). Horror melodrama. Newlyweds become prisoners of a demonic Satanist but are befriended by his mortal enemy. *Sc:* Peter Ruric and Edgar G. Ulmer (from story by Edgar Allan Poe). *Ph:* John Mescal. *Art dir:* Charles D. Hall. *Ed:* Ray Curtiss. *Mus:* Heinz Roemheld. *With:* Karloff (*Hjalmar Poelzig*), Bela Lugosi (*Dr. Vitus Verdegast*), David Manners (*Peter Allison*), Jacqueline Wells (*Joan Allison*), Lucille Lund (*Karen*), Egon Brecher (*Majordomo*), Anna Duncan (*maid*), Henry Armetta, Albert Conti, Herman Bing, Harry Cording, George Davis. *Prod:* Carl Laemmle for Universal Pictures. 65m.

THUNDER OVER TEXAS (1934). Western. A girl is orphaned when her father is killed for valuable maps; later she is abducted and rescued. *Dir:* John Warner. *Sc:* Eddie Granemann (story by Shirley Castle). *Ph:* Harry Forbes. *Ed:* George Merrick. *With:* Big Boy Williams (*Ted Wright*), Marion Shilling (*Helen Mason*), Helen Westcott (*Tiny*), Claude Dayton (*Bruce Laird*), Philo McCullough, Robert McKenzie, Tiny Skelton. A Beacon Production. 50m. Ulmer directed this film under the pseudonym of John Warner to prevent Universal from discovering that he was also working elsewhere. Shirley Castle is the maiden name of Ulmer's wife.

GREEN FIELDS (1937). Talmudic student leaves synagogue to experience life in the country and is adopted by a family that wants him to marry their daughter. *Co-dir:* Jacob Ben-Ami. *Sc:* George G. Mascor and Peretz Hirshbein (from play by Peretz Hirshbein). *Ph:* William Miller and Burgi Contner. *Mus:* Vladimir Heifitz. *With:* Michael Goldstein (*Levy-Yitzchok*), Helen Beverly (*Izineh*), Isidore Cashier (*David-Noich*), Anna Appel (*Rochel*), Lea Noimi (*Gittel*), Dena Drute (*Stera*), Max Vodnoy, Saul Levine, Hershel Benardi. *Prod:* Edgar G. Ulmer for Creative Film Producers. Released by New Star Film Co. Over two hours in length. In Yiddish.

THE SINGING BLACKSMITH (1938). Musical. An unsophisticated village blacksmith marries but still has difficulties with an old girl friend. *Sc:* Ben-Zvi Baratoff and Ossip Dymow (based on play by David Pinski). *With:* Moishe Oysher (*Yankel*), Miriam Riselle (*Tamara*), Florence Weiss (*Rivke*), Anna Appel (*Chaya-Pesche*), Ben-Zvi Baratoff (*Bendet*), Michael Goldstein (*Raffuel*), Lea Noimi (*Mariashe*), Max Vodnoy (*Simche*). *Prod:* Edgar G. Ulmer for Collective Film Producers. Released by New Star Film Co. In Yiddish.

MOON OVER HARLEM (1939). *Sc:* Shirley Castle (story by Mathew Mathews). Released by Meteor Productions, Inc. 8 reels.

THE LIGHT AHEAD (1939). A cholera epidemic in an 1880's, poverty-stricken Polish village is blamed on a blind girl's violation of the Sabbath; to appease evil spirits she is forced to marry the village cripple in a ceremony performed in a cemetery. *Sc:* Chaver-Paver (story by S. J. Abramowitz). *With:* Izidore Casher (*Mendel*), Helen Beverly (*Hodel*), David Opatoshu (*Fishke*), Yudel Dubinsky (*Isaac*), Rosetta Bialis (*Dropke*), Tillie Rabinowitz, Misha Fishman, Leon Seidenberg, Anna Guskin. *Prod:* Edgar G. Ulmer for Ultra Film Productions. Approximately two hours in length. In Yiddish. Yiddish title is DI KLIATSHE.

COSSACKS IN EXILE (1939). Musical romance. Love story set against the flight of Ukrainian cossacks to Turkey and their return to their native land. *Sc:* based on operetta by S. Artemovsky. *With:* Maria Sokill (*Odarka*), Michael Shvets (*Ivan*), Helen Orlenko (*Oxana*), Alexis Tcherkassky (*Andrey*), Nicholas Karlash (*Sultan*), Vladimir Sikevitch, Vladimir Zelitsky, D. Creona. *Prod:* V. Avramenko. In Ukrainian. Ukrainian title is ZAPOROZHETS ZA DUNAYEM.

AMERICAN MATCHMAKER (1940). Melodrama. Mother wants her daughter to find a husband through a matchmaking bureau. *With:* Judith Abarbanel, Rosetta Bialis, Leo Fuchs, Yudel Dubinsky, Abe Lax. *Prod:* Edgar G. Ulmer for Fame Films. In Yiddish.

CLOUD IN THE SKY (1940). Health documentary. An illustration in Spanish and English of the importance of early diagnosis and treatment of tuberculosis. *Sc:* H. E. Kleinschmidt. Released by the National Tuberculosis and Health Association. 18m.

ANOTHER TO CONQUER (1941). Health documentary. A discussion of the dangers of tuberculosis. *Sc:* Harry E. Kleinschmidt. Released by the National Tuberculosis and Health Association. 20m.

LET MY PEOPLE LIVE (1942). Health documentary. A discussion of tuberculosis and the Negro race made at Tuskegee Institute in Alabama. *With:* Rex Ingram, Peggy Howard, Erostine Coles, Earl Brown. Released by the National Tuberculosis and Health Association. 25m.

TOMORROW WE LIVE (1942). Mystery melodrama. A girl discovers that her father is mysteriously controlled by a Las Vegas gambler and almost falls under his control herself. *Sc:* Bert Lytton. *Ph:* Jack Greenhalgh. *Art dir:* Fred Preble. *Ed:* Dan Milner. *Mus:* Leo Erdody. *With:* Ricardo Cortez (*the Ghost*), Jean Parker (*Julie*), Emmett Lynn (*Pop Bronson*), William Marshall (*Lt. Bob Ford*), Roseanne Stevens (*Melba*), Ray Miller, Frank S. Hagney, Rex Lease, Jack Ingram. *Prod:* Seymour Nebenzal for P.R.C.

MY SON, THE HERO (1943). *Sc:* Edgar G. Ulmer and Doris Malloy. *Ph:* Jack Greenhalgh and Robert Cline. *Ed:* Charles Henkel, Jr. *Mus:* Leo Erdody. *With:* Patsy Kelly, Roscoe Karns, Joan Blair, Carol Hughes. *Prod:* Peter R. Van Duinen for P.R.C. 7 reels.

GIRLS IN CHAINS (1943). Melodrama. Woman takes job in school for delinquent girls to get evidence on corrupt racketeer. *Sc:* Albert Beich (story by Edgar G. Ulmer). *Ph:* Ira Morgan. *Art dir:* Fred Preble. *Ed:* Charles Henkel, Jr. *Mus:* Leo Erdody. *With:* Arlene Judge (*Helen*), Roger Clark (*Frank Donovan*), Robin Raymond (*Rita*), Barbara Pepper (*Ruth*), Dorothy Burgess (*Mrs. Peters*), Clancy Cooper (*Marcus*), Allen Byron (*Johnny Moon*). *Prod:* Peter R. Van Duinen for P.R.C. 7 reels.

ISLE OF FORGOTTEN SINS (1943). Adventure melodrama. Two deep-sea divers and a boatful of women try to salvage a sunken shipment of gold. *Sc:* Raymond L. Schrock (story by Edgar

THE HOLLYWOOD PROFESSIONALS

G. Ulmer). *Ph:* Ira Morgan. *Art dir:* Fred Preble. *Ed:* Charles Henkel, Jr. *Mus:* Leo Erdody. *With:* John Carradine (*Clancy*), Gale Sondergaard (*Marge*), Sidney Toler (*Krogan*), Frank Fenton (*Burke*), Veda Ann Borg (*Luana*), Rita Quigley (*Diane*), Rick Vallin (*Johnny Pacific*), Tala Birell, Patti McCarthy, Betty Amann, Marian Colby, William Edmonds. *Prod:* Peter R. Van Duinen for P.R.C. 86m. Also titled MONSOON.

JIVE JUNCTION (1943). Musical. Talented young bandleader makes national champs out of high school band. *Sc:* Irving Wallace, Walter Doniger and Marvin Wald (story by Marvin Wald and Walter Doniger). *Ph:* Ira Morgan. *Ed:* Robert Crandall. *Mus:* Leo Erdody. *With:* Dickie Moore (*Peter*), Tina Thayer (*Claire*), Gerra Young (*Gerra*), Johnny Michaels (*Jimmy*), Jack Wagner (*Grant*), Jan Wiley (*Miss Forbes*), Beverly Boyd (*Cubby*). Released by P.R.C. 64m.

BLUEBEARD (1944). Melodrama. An artist paints women, then strangles them. *Sc:* Pierre Gendron (story by Arnold Phillips and Werner H. Furst). *Ph:* Jockey A. Feindell (supervised by Eugen Schufftan). *Art dir:* Paul Palmentola. *Ed:* Carl Pierson. *Mus:* Leo Erdody. *With:* John Carradine (*Gaston Morel*), Jean Parker (*Lucille*), Nils Asther, Ludwig Stossel, George Pembroke, Teala Loring, Sonia Sorel, Henry Kolker, Emmett Lynn, Iris Adrian, Patti McCarthy, Carrie Devan, Anne Sterling. *Prod:* Leon Fromkess for P.R.C. 73m.

STRANGE ILLUSION (1945). Mystery melodrama. A young man's nightmare starts to come true. *Sc:* Adele Comandini (story by Fritz Rotter). *Ph:* Philip Tannura. *Art dir:* Paul Palmentola. *Ed:* Carl Pierson. *Mus:* Leo Erdody. *With:* James Lydon (*Paul Cartwright*), Sally Eilers (*Virginia Cartwright*), Warren William (*Brett Curtis*), Regis Toomey (*Dr. Vincent*), Charles Arnt (*Professor Muhlbach*), George H. Reed (*Benjamin*), Jayne Hazard (*Dorothy Cartwright*), Jimmy Clark, Mary McLeod, Pierre Watkin, Sonia Sorel, Vic Potel. *Prod:* Leon Fromkess for P.R.C. 80m. Also titled OUT OF THE NIGHT.

CLUB HAVANA (1945). Melodrama. Six separate stories intersect and climax at the Club Havana on a single evening. *Sc:* Raymond L. Schrock (story by Fred L. Jackson). *Ph:* Benjamin N. Kline. *Art dir:* Edward C. Jewell. *Ed:* Carl Pierson. *Mus:* Howard Jackson. *With:* Tom Neal (*Bill Porter*), Margaret Lindsay (*Rosalind*), Don Douglas (*Johnny Norton*), Isabelita (*Herself*), Dorothy Morris (*Lucy*), Ernest Truex (*Willy Kingston*), Renie Riano (*Mrs. Cavendish*), Gertrude Mitchell (*Hetty*), Carlos Molina and his music of the Americas. Released by P.R.C. 62m.

DETOUR (1946). Psychological melodrama. New York piano player hitchhikes to California and becomes involved in murder. *Sc:* Martin Goldsmith. *Ph:* Benjamin Kline. *Art dir:* Edward C. Jewell. *Ed:* George McGuire. *Mus:* Leo Erdody. *With:* Tom Neal (*Al Roberts*), Ann Savage (*Vera*), Claudia Drake (*Sue*), Edmund MacDonald (*Charles Haskell, Jr.*), Tim Ryan, Esther Howard, Pat Gleason. *Prod:* Leon Fromkess for P.R.C. 69m.

THE WIFE OF MONTE CRISTO (1946). Melodrama. The Avenger battles a drug syndicate that would endan-

DETOUR: the lights go down and Ulmer dollies in to close-up, to suggest that Roberts's (Tom Neal) story is mental experience. Frame enlargement

ger the health of citizens in 1830's Paris. *Sc:* Dorcas Cochran (story by Franz Rosenwald and Edgar G. Ulmer suggested by novel by Alexandre Dumas). *Ph:* Adolph Edward Kull. *Art dir:* Edward C. Jewell. *Ed:* Douglas Bagier. *Mus:* Paul Dessau. *With:* John Loder (*De Villefort*), Lenore Aubert (*Haydée*), Martin Kosleck (*Count of Monte Cristo*), Charles Dingle (*Danglars*), Eduardo Ciannelli (*Antoine*), Fritz Feld (*Bonnet*), Eva Gabor (*Madame Maillard*), Fritz Kortner (*Maillard*). *Prod:* Leon Fromkess for P.R.C. 80m.

HER SISTER'S SECRET (1946). Melodrama. Girl has second thoughts about giving her fatherless child to her childless sister. *Sc:* Anne Green (based on novel by Gina Kaus). *Ph:* Frank F. Planer. *Art dir:* Edward C. Jewell. *Ed:*

Jack W. Ogilvie. *Mus:* Hans Sommer. *With:* Nancy Coleman (*Toni Dubois*), Margaret Lindsay (*Renée Dubois*), Philip Reed (*Dick Connolly*), Regis Toomey (*Bill Gordon*), Henry Stephenson (*Mr. Dubois*), Felix Bressart (*Pepe*), Winston Severn, Fritz Feld. *Prod:* Henry Brash for P.R.C. 85m.

THE STRANGE WOMAN (1946). Melodrama. A New England *femme fatale* destroys the men who love her, gaining wealth but losing her soul. *Sc:* Herb Meadow (from novel by Ben Ames Williams). *Ph:* Lucien Andriot. *Ed:* James E. Newcom. *Mus:* Carmen Dragon. *With:* Hedy Lamarr (*Jenny Hager*), George Sanders (*John Evered*), Louis Hayward (*Ephraim Poster*), Gene Lockhart (*Isaiah Poster*), Hillary Brooke (*Meg Saladine*), Rhys Williams (*Deacon Adams*), June Storey, Moroni Olson, Olive Blakeney, Alan Napier, Dennis Hoey. *Prod:* Jack Chertok for United Artists (A Hunt Stromberg Presentation). 100m.

CARNEGIE HALL (1947). Musical melodrama. Mother works as custodian at Carnegie Hall to get her son a musical education. *Sc:* Karl Kamb (story by Seena Owen). *Ph:* William Miller. *With:* Marsha Hunt (*Nora Ryan*), William Prince (*Tony Salerno Jr.*), Frank McHugh (*John Donovan*), Martha O'Driscoll (*Ruth Haines*), Hans Yaray (*Tony Salerno Sr.*), Joseph Buloff (*Anton Tribik*), Bruno Walter, Lily Pons, Gregor Piatigorsky, Rise Stevens, Artur Rodzinski, Artur Rubinstein, Jan Peerce, Ezio Pinza, Jascha Heifetz and others. *Prod:* Boris Morros and William LeBarron for United Artists. 134m.

RUTHLESS (1948). Man destroys his

friends and loved ones in his pursuit of wealth and success. *Sc:* S. K. Lauren and Gordon Kahn (from novel by Dayton Stoddart). *Ph:* Bert Glennon. *Art dir:* Frank Sylos. *Ed:* Francis D. Lyon. *Mus:* Werner Janssen. *With:* Zachary Scott (*Horace Woodruff Vendig*), Louis Hayward (*Vic Lambdin*), Diana Lynn (*Martha Burnside/Mallory Flagg*), Sydney Greenstreet (*Buck Mansfield*), Lucile Bremer (*Christa Mansfield*), Martha Vickers (*Susan Duane*), Edith Barrett, Dennis Hoey, Raymond Burr, Joyce Arling. *Prod:* Arthur S. Lyons for Eagle Lion Films. 104m.

THE PIRATES OF CAPRI (1949). Period adventure. Pirate frees people of Capri from a despotic police commissioner. *Sc:* S. Alexander (story by G. Colonna, G. Moser and B. Valeri). *Ph:* Anchise Brizzi. *Art dir:* G. Fiorini. *Ed:* R. Lucidi. *Mus:* Nino Rota. *With:* Louis Hayward (*Capt. Sirocco/Count Amalfi*), Binnie Barnes (*Queen Caroline*), Mariella Lotti (*Countess Mercedes*), Rudolph Serato (*Von Holstein*), Alan Curtis (*Commodore Van Diel*), Michael Rasumney (*Pepino*), Virginia Belmont (*Annette*). *Prod:* Victor Pahlen. 94m. Also titled CAPTAIN SIROCCO.

ST. BENNY THE DIP (1951). Comedy. Three con men escape police by dressing as priests in stolen ecclestiastical garments and open church on the Bowery to protect their identity. *Sc:* John Roeburt (story by George Auerbach). *Ph:* Don Malkamus. *Mus:* Robert Stringer. *With:* Dick Haymes (*Benny*), Nina Foch (*Linda Kovacs*), Roland Young (*Matthew*), Lionel Stander (*Monk*), Freddie Bartholomew (*Rev. Wilbur*), Oscar Karlweis, Dort Clark, Will Lee.

Prod: Edward J. and Harry Lee Danziger for United Artists. 81m.

THE MAN FROM PLANET X (1951). Science fiction. Planet that is slowly freezing sends scout to Earth for resettlement programme there. *Sc:* Aubrey Wisberg and Jack Pollexfen. *Ph:* John L. Russell. *Mus:* Charles Koff. *With:* Robert Clarke (*Lawrence*), Margaret Field (*Enid*), Raymond Bond (*Professor Elliot*), William Schallert (*Mears*), Roy Engel, Charles Davis, Gilbert Fallman, David Ormont. *Prod:* Aubrey Wisberg and Jack Pollexfen for United Artists. 70m.

BABES IN BAGDAD (1952). Comedy. Caliph's son proves woman is man's equal by helping members of a harem outwit their husband. *Sc:* Felix Feist and Joe Anson. *Ph:* Jack Cox (Cinefotocolor). *Ed:* Edith Lenny. *Mus:* J. Leoz. *With:* Paulette Goddard (*Kyra*), Gypsy Rose Lee (*Zohara*), John Boles (*Hassan*), Richard Ney (*Ezar*), Thomas Gallagher (*Sharkhan*), Sebastian Cabot (*Sinbad*), Carmen Sevilla, MacDonald Parke, Natalie Benesh, Hugh Dempster. *Prod:* Edward J. and Harry Lee Danziger for Danziger Productions. 79m.

NAKED DAWN (1955). Western. Bandit corrupts young Mexican farmer and plots to steal his wife. *Sc:* Nina and Herman Schneider. *Ph:* Frederick Gately (Technicolor). *Art dir:* Martin Lencer. *Ed:* Dan Milner. *Mus:* Herschel Burke Gilbert. *With:* Arthur Kennedy (*Santiago*), Betta St. John (*Maria*), Eugene Iglesias (*Manuel*), Roy Engel (*Guntz*). *Prod:* James O. Radford for Universal International. 82m.

MURDER IS MY BEAT (1955). Mystery. Girl convicted of murder sees man alive she is supposed to have killed. *Sc:* Aubrey Wisberg (story by Aubrey Wisberg and Martin Field). *Ph:* Harold E. Wellman. *Art dir:* James Sullivan and Harry H. Reif. *Ed:* Fred H. Feitshans, Jr. *Mus:* Al Glasser. *With:* Paul Langton (*Ray*), Barbara Payton (*Eden Lane*), Robert Shayne (*Bert*), Selena Royle, Roy Gordon, Tracy Roberts, Kate McKenna, Henry W. Harvey, Sr., Jay Adler. *Prod:* Aubrey Wisberg for Allied Artists. 77m. Also titled DYNAMITE ANCHORAGE.

THE DAUGHTER OF DR. JEKYLL (1957). Horror. Girl believes that she, like her notorious father, is a werewolf. *Sc:* Jack Pollexfen. *Ph:* John F. Warren (widescreen). *Art dir:* Mowbray Berkeley. *Ed:* Holbrook N. Todd. *Mus:* Melvyn Lenard. *With:* John Agar (*George Hastings*), Gloria Talbot (*Janet Smith*), Arthur Shields (*Dr. Lomas*), John Dierkes (*Jacob*), Mollie McCart (*Maggie*), Martha Wentworth (*Mrs. Merchant*), Marjorie Stapp, Rita Greene, Marel Page. *Prod:* Jack Pollexfen for Allied Artists (A Film Ventures Production). 74m.

HANNIBAL (1960). Historical epic. Hannibal crosses the Alps to attack Rome. *Sc:* Mortimer Braus (story by Ottavio Poggi). *Ph:* R. Masciocchi (Technicolor, SuperCinescope). *Art dir:* E. Kromberg. *Ed:* R. Cinquini. *Mus:* Carlo Rustichelli and Franco Ferrara. *With:* Victor Mature (*Hannibal*), Rita Gam (*Sylvia*), Milly Vitale (*Daniella*), Gabriel Ferzetti (*Fabius*), Rik Battaglia (*Hasdrubal*), Franco Silva (*Maharbal*). *Prod:* Ottavio Poggi for Warner Bros. 103m.

THE AMAZING TRANSPARENT MAN (1960). Science fiction. Mad scientist uses serum that makes things transparent to plot a bank robbery and later attain world power. *Sc:* Jack Lewis. *Ph:* Meredith M. Nicholson. *Art dir:* Ernest Fegte and Louise Caldwell. *Ed:* Jack Ruggiero. *Mus:* Darrell Calker. *With:* Marguerite Chapman (*Laura*), Douglas Kennedy (*Joey Faust*), James Griffith (*Krenner*), Ivan Triesault (*Dr. Ulof*), Red Morgan (*Julian*), Carmel Daniel (*Maria*), Edward Erwin (*Drake*), Jonathan Ledford (*Smith*). *Prod:* John Miller, Robert L. Madden and Lester D. Guthrie for American International. 60m.

BEYOND THE TIME BARRIER (1960). Science fiction. An Air Force pilot breaks the time barrier and lands in 2024 A.D. *Sc:* Arthur G. Pierce. *Ph:* Meredith M. Nicholson. *Art dir:* Ernst Fegte. *Ed:* Jack Ruggiero. *Mus:* Darrell Calker. *With:* Robert Clarke (*Major William Allison*), Darlene Tompkins (*Trirene*), Arianne Arden (*Markova*), Vladimir Sokoloff (*The Supreme*), Stephen Bekassy (*Karl Kruse*), John van Dreelen (*Dr. Bourman*), Red Morgan, Ken Knox. *Prod:* John Miles, Robert L. Madden and Robert Clarke for American International. 75m.

L'ATLANTIDE (1961). Two engineers find the lost city of Atlantis. *With:* Haya Harareet, Jean-Louis Trintignant, Rod Fulton, Georges Rivière, Amadeo Nazzari, Giulia Rubini. Released by Avco-Embassy Pictures. 105m. The film was begun by Frank Borzage who directed for only a few days; it was re-written and re-shot by Ulmer after Borzage became ill. Also titled QUEEN OF ATLANTIS and JOURNEY BENEATH THE DESERT.

THE CAVERN (1965). War melodrama. Six men and a woman are trapped in an Italian cave for several months during the Second World War. *Sc:* Michael Pertwee and Jack Davies. *Ph:* Gabor Pogany (widescreen). *Ed:* Renato Cinquini. *Mus:* Carlo Rustichelli and Franco Ferrara. *With:* John Saxon (*Kramer*), Rosanna Schiaffino (*Anna*), Larry Hagman (*Capt. Wilson*), Peter L. Marshall (*Peter Carter*), Nino Castelnuovo (*Mario*), Brian Aherne (*General Braithwaite*), Hans von Borsody (*Hans*), Joachim Hansen (*German Sergeant*). *Prod:* Edgar G. Ulmer for 20th Century-Fox. 96m.

Design by Ulmer for the ill-fated Mary Queen of Scots project he began in Italy with Hedy Lamarr and had to abandon when the star disappeared. Courtesy of Mrs. Ulmer

Index to Names